Classics

THE AUSTRALIAN
Women's Weekly

Contents

There are times when you just want to make the most basic recipe with no frills, no twists, nothing exotic added, just something wonderfully classic. Perhaps you've recalled a particular cake from your childhood, a hearty wintry soup from a cookbook, or you have memories of a delicious recipe you've cooked that originally came from another country. This cookbook is full of such recipes, all classic, unadorned, but just sensational.

Pamela Clark

Food Director

Introduction

Many things come and go, but the pleasure of eating isn't one of them. With fashions in food changing so much it's comforting to turn back to the old favourites. The aroma of a traditional Sunday roast wafting from the oven can instantly take you back in time to your childhood. The classics are those tried and true dishes that you know taste great – the ones that have stood the test of time and appear on your dining table time and time again.

To experience a true classic like boeuf bourguignon, chicken cacciatore or paella is to connect with the past, and to feel a sense of continuity with history. There's something quite respectful, not to mention reassuring, about cooking food that generations of different cultures have perfected and relished.

Once you've mastered these classics you can start to experiment with them – adapt them to suit what's in the cupboard, what's in season or give them a modern twist. You need to know the rules before you can break them. But often, you won't want to.

Classic
Breakfasts

creamy scrambled eggs

prep + cook time 20 minutes **serves** 4

8 eggs
½ cup (125ml) cream
2 tablespoons finely chopped fresh chives
30g butter

1 Place eggs, cream and chives in medium bowl; beat lightly with fork.

2 Heat butter in large frying pan over medium heat. Add egg mixture, wait a few seconds, then use a wide spatula to gently scrape the set egg mixture along the base of the pan; cook until creamy and barely set. Serve immediately, with toast, if you like.

nutritional count per serving 30.2g total fat (16.2g saturated fat); 1375kJ (329 cal); 1.3g carbohydrate; 14g protein; 0g fibre

herb omelette with sautéed mushrooms

prep + cook time 30 minutes **serves** 4

2 tablespoons finely chopped fresh flat-leaf parsley
2 tablespoons finely chopped fresh chervil
2 tablespoons finely chopped fresh chives
2 tablespoons finely chopped fresh tarragon
50g butter
2 tablespoons olive oil
250g swiss brown mushrooms, halved
½ cup (125ml) water
2 teaspoons finely grated lemon rind
1 tablespoon lemon juice
12 eggs

1 Combine herbs in small bowl.
2 Heat 30g of the butter and 1 tablespoon of the oil in large frying pan. Add mushrooms; cook, stirring, 5 minutes. Stir in 2 tablespoons of the water; cook, stirring, until water evaporates and mushrooms are tender. Remove from heat; stir in rind, juice and 2 tablespoons of the herb mixture. Cover to keep warm.
3 Gently whisk eggs and remaining water in large bowl; whisk in remaining herb mixture.
4 Heat a quarter of the remaining butter and 1 teaspoon of the remaining oil in medium frying pan. When butter mixture bubbles, pour a quarter of the egg mixture into pan; cook over medium heat, tilting pan, until egg is almost set. Tilt pan backwards; fold omelette in half. Cook 30 seconds then slide onto serving plate.
5 Repeat step 4, wiping out pan before each addition to make a total of 4 omelettes. Serve omelettes topped with sautéed mushrooms.

nutritional count per serving 35.3g total fat (12.9g saturated fat); 1718kJ (411 cal); 1g carbohydrate; 22.5g protein; 2g fibre

salmon kedgeree

prep + cook time 25 minutes **serves** 6

1½ cups (300g) white long-grain rice

415g can red salmon

80g butter

⅓ cup coarsely chopped fresh flat-leaf parsley

2 teaspoons lemon juice

3 hard-boiled eggs, chopped coarsely

1 Cook rice in large saucepan of boiling water until tender; drain.

2 Drain salmon; discard skin and bones. Flake flesh.

3 Melt butter in large frying pan; add rice, parsley and juice. Cook, stirring, until heated through. Add salmon and eggs; cook, stirring gently, until heated through. Serve with lemon wedges, if you like.

nutritional count per serving 20.5g total fat (9.9g saturated fat); 1760kJ (421 cal); 39.7g carbohydrate; 19.1g protein; 0.6g fibre

You can use leftover cooked rice, if you have some; you'll need about 5 cups.

corn fritters

prep + cook time 40 minutes **makes** 18

1 cup (150g) self-raising flour

½ teaspoon bicarbonate of soda

1 teaspoon ground cumin

¾ cup (180ml) milk

2 eggs, separated

2 cups (330g) fresh corn kernels

2 green onions, sliced finely

2 tablespoons finely chopped fresh coriander

1 Sift flour, soda and cumin into medium bowl. Gradually whisk in milk and egg yolks until batter is smooth.

2 Beat egg whites in small bowl with electric mixer until soft peaks form.

3 Stir corn, onion and coriander into batter; fold in egg whites.

4 Pour 2 tablespoons of the batter for each fritter into heated oiled large frying pan; spread batter into round shape. Cook fritters about 2 minutes each side. Remove from pan; cover to keep warm.

5 Repeat step 4 to make a total of 18 fritters. Fritters can be served with tomato chutney and fresh coriander leaves.

nutritional count per fritter 1.3g total fat (0.5g saturated fat); 263kJ (63 cal); 9.9g carbohydrate; 2.7g protein; 1.2g fibre

You can substitute 425g can corn kernels, rinsed and drained, for the fresh corn kernels, if you like.

blueberry pancakes with bacon

prep + cook time 35 minutes **serves** 6

2 cups (300g) self-raising flour

¼ cup (55g) caster sugar

2 eggs

600ml buttermilk

50g butter, melted

1 cup (150g) fresh blueberries

12 thin bacon rashers (360g), rind removed

½ cup (125ml) maple syrup

1 Sift flour and sugar into medium bowl.

2 Whisk eggs, buttermilk and butter in large jug. Gradually whisk egg mixture into flour mixture until smooth. Stir in blueberries; pour batter into large jug.

3 Pour ¼-cup batter for each pancake into heated oiled large frying pan. Cook pancakes until bubbles appear on the surface; turn, brown other side. Cover to keep warm.

4 Repeat step 3 to make a total of 18 pancakes.

5 Meanwhile, heat oiled large frying pan; cook bacon until crisp. Drizzle pancakes with syrup, serve with bacon.

nutritional count per serving 19.3g total fat (9.4g saturated fat); 2345kJ (561 cal); 71.8g carbohydrate; 23.3g protein; 2.4g fibre

french toast

prep + cook time 20 minutes **serves** 4

4 eggs
½ cup (125ml) cream
¼ cup (60ml) milk
1 teaspoon ground cinnamon
¼ cup (55g) caster sugar
100g butter, melted
8 thick slices white bread (360g)
2 tablespoons icing sugar
⅓ cup (80ml) maple syrup

1 Whisk eggs in medium bowl, then whisk in cream, milk, cinnamon and sugar.
2 Heat a quarter of the butter in medium frying pan. Dip two bread slices into egg mixture, one at a time; cook bread until browned both sides. Remove french toast from pan; keep warm.
3 Repeat step 2 to make a total of 8 french toasts.
4 Serve toasts dusted with sifted icing sugar and drizzled with maple syrup. Top with sliced strawberries, if you like.

nutritional count per serving 42.2g total fat (24.8g saturated fat); 3194kJ (764 cal); 79.4g carbohydrate; 15.5g protein; 2.6g fibre

cooked english breakfast

prep + cook time 20 minutes **serves** 4

50g butter

300g button mushrooms, halved

8 chipolata sausages (240g)

4 rindless bacon rashers (260g)

2 medium tomatoes (300g), halved

1 tablespoon vegetable oil

8 eggs

1 Melt butter in medium saucepan; cook mushrooms, stirring, about 5 minutes or until tender.

2 Cook sausages and bacon in heated oiled large frying pan. Remove from pan; cover to keep warm. Drain fat from pan.

3 Preheat grill. Place tomato, cut-side up, on oven tray; grill tomato until browned lightly.

4 Meanwhile, heat oil in same large frying pan, add eggs; cook eggs until done to your liking.

5 Serve mushrooms, sausages, bacon, tomato and eggs with toast, if you like.

nutritional count per serving 47.7g total fat (20.2g saturated fat); 2424kJ (580 cal); 3.5g carbohydrate; 34.6g protein; 2.4g fibre

eggs benedict

prep + cook time 50 minutes **serves** 4

8 eggs

4 english muffins

200g shaved leg ham

¼ cup finely chopped fresh chives

hollandaise sauce

1½ tablespoons white wine vinegar

1 tablespoon lemon juice

½ teaspoon black peppercorns

2 egg yolks

125g unsalted butter, melted

1 Make hollandaise sauce.

2 To poach eggs, half-fill a large shallow frying pan with water; bring to the boil. Break 1 egg into a cup, then slide into pan; repeat with three more eggs. When all eggs are in pan, allow water to return to the boil. Cover pan, turn off heat; stand about 4 minutes or until a light film of egg white sets over yolks. Remove the egg with a slotted spoon and drain on absorbent paper; cover to keep warm. Repeat with remaining eggs.

3 Meanwhile, split muffins in half and toast. Serve muffins topped with ham, poached eggs, sauce and chives.

hollandaise sauce Combine vinegar, juice and peppercorns in small saucepan; bring to the boil. Reduce heat; simmer, uncovered, until liquid is reduced by half. Strain through a fine sieve into small heatproof bowl; cool 10 minutes. Whisk egg yolks into vinegar mixture. Set bowl over small saucepan of simmering water; do not allow water to touch base of bowl. Whisk mixture over heat until thickened. Remove bowl from heat; gradually whisk in melted butter in a thin steady stream, whisking constantly until sauce is thick and creamy.

nutritional count per serving 40.6g total fat (21.2g saturated fat); 2450kJ (586 cal); 24.2g carbohydrate; 30.8g protein; 2g fibre

bircher muesli

prep time 20 minutes (+ refrigeration) **serves** 6

2 cups (180g) rolled oats

1¼ cups (310ml) apple juice

1 cup (280g) yogurt

2 medium (300g) apples

¼ cup (35g) roasted slivered almonds

¼ cup (40g) currants

¼ cup (20g) toasted shredded coconut

1 teaspoon ground cinnamon

½ cup (140g) yogurt, extra

1 Combine oats, juice and yogurt in medium bowl. Cover; refrigerate overnight.

2 Peel, core and coarsely grate one apple; stir into oat mixture with nuts, currants, coconut and cinnamon.

3 Core and thinly slice remaining apple. Serve muesli topped with extra yogurt and apple slices.

nutritional count per serving 10.4g total fat (4.1g saturated fat); 1187kJ (284 cal); 37g carbohydrate; 8.2g protein; 4.3g fibre

overnight bran muffins

prep + cook time 30 minutes (+ refrigeration) **makes** 12

1 egg

1¼ cups (185g) plain flour

1 teaspoon ground cinnamon

1 teaspoon bicarbonate of soda

½ cup (110g) firmly packed brown sugar

1¾ cups (105g) unprocessed bran

¾ cup (105g) coarsely chopped seedless fresh
   or dried dates

1½ cups (375ml) buttermilk

½ cup (125ml) vegetable oil

1 Whisk egg in medium bowl, stir in remaining ingredients. (Do not over-mix; mixture should be lumpy.) Cover mixture, refrigerate overnight.

2 Preheat oven to 200°C/180°C fan-forced. Grease 12-hole (⅓-cup/80ml) muffin pan.

3 Spoon mixture into pan holes; bake about 20 minutes. Stand muffins in pan 5 minutes before turning, top-side up, onto wire rack to cool. Serve with butter, if you like.

nutritional count per muffin 11.3g total fat (1.9g saturated fat); 1037kJ (248 cal); 28.7g carbohydrate; 5.2g protein; 5.3g fibre

Classic
Starters

prawn cocktail

prep time 30 minutes **serves** 4

32 cooked medium prawns (1.5g)

⅓ cup (100g) mayonnaise

2 tablespoons cream

1 tablespoon tomato sauce

1 teaspoon worcestershire sauce

½ teaspoon Tabasco sauce

½ teaspoon dijon mustard

2 teaspoons lemon juice

½ iceberg lettuce, shredded finely

4 lemon wedges

1 Shell and devein prawns.

2 Whisk mayonnaise, cream, sauces, mustard and juice in small bowl.

3 Divide lettuce among serving glasses; top with prawns and sauce. Serve with lemon wedges.

nutritional count per serving 14.2g total fat (4.2g saturated fat); 1254kJ (300 cal); 7.6g carbohydrate; 34.6g protein; 1.8g fibre

chicken liver pâté

prep + cook time 45 minutes (+ refrigeration) **makes** 4 cups

1kg chicken livers
200g ghee (clarified butter)
4 rindless bacon rashers (260g)
1 small brown onion (80g), chopped finely
¼ cup (60ml) brandy
½ cup (125ml) cream
2 teaspoons finely chopped fresh thyme
pinch ground nutmeg

1 Cut any sinew from livers; pull each lobe away from connecting tissue.
2 Heat a quarter of the ghee in large frying pan; cook half the livers, stirring, until browned and barely cooked. Remove from pan. Repeat with another quarter of the ghee and remaining livers.
3 Heat 1 tablespoon of the remaining ghee in same pan; cook bacon and onion, stirring, until onion softens. Add brandy; bring to the boil.
4 Blend livers, bacon mixture, cream, thyme, nutmeg and 2 tablespoons of the remaining ghee until smooth (you may need to do this in batches).
5 Press pâté into 1-litre (4-cup) dish; melt remaining ghee, pour over pâté in dish. Refrigerate 3 hours or overnight. Serve with melba toasts or water crackers, if you like.

---

nutritional count per teaspoon 1.7g total fat
(1g saturated fat); 88kJ (21 cal);
0.1g carbohydrate; 1.2g protein; 0g fibre

coquilles saint jacques

prep + cook time 45 minutes **serves** 4

1½ cups (375ml) chicken stock

1 cup (250ml) dry white wine

2 shallots (50g), chopped finely

750g scallops, without roe

250g button mushrooms, sliced thinly

50g butter

2 tablespoons plain flour

½ cup (125ml) milk

½ cup (125ml) cream

2 egg yolks

2 teaspoons lemon juice

1 cup (70g) stale breadcrumbs

2 tablespoons finely grated swiss cheese

1 tablespoon finely chopped fresh chives

30g butter, melted, extra

1 Bring stock, wine and shallots to the boil in medium saucepan; reduce heat. Add scallops and mushrooms; simmer 2 minutes or until scallops are barely cooked. Remove scallops and mushrooms with a slotted spoon.

2 Bring poaching liquid to the boil; boil 5 minutes or until reduced to ½ cup. Strain into heatproof bowl; reserve liquid.

3 Melt butter in small saucepan; add flour. Cook, stirring, until mixture bubbles and thickens. Gradually stir in combined milk, cream and reserved poaching liquid. Cook, stirring, until mixture boils and thickens. Remove from heat; whisk in egg yolks and juice.

4 Combine breadcrumbs, cheese, chives and extra butter in medium bowl. Divide scallops and mushrooms among four 1-cup (250ml) gratin dishes; spoon over sauce. Sprinkle with breadcrumb mixture. Cook scallops under a preheated grill until browned lightly.

nutritional count per serving 38.8g total fat (23.5g saturated fat); 2558kJ (612 cal); 21.1g carbohydrate; 33.9g protein; 2.7g fibre

terrine de campagne

prep + cook time 2 hours 20 minutes (+ refrigeration) **serves** 6

350g chicken thigh fillets, chopped coarsely

400g boned pork belly, rind removed, chopped coarsely

300g calves' liver, trimmed, chopped coarsely

3 rindless bacon rashers (195g), chopped coarsely

3 cloves garlic, crushed

2 teaspoons finely chopped fresh thyme

10 juniper berries, crushed

2 tablespoons port

¼ cup (60ml) dry white wine

1 egg, beaten lightly

1 Preheat oven to 150°C/130°C fan-forced. Oil 1.5-litre (6-cup) ovenproof terrine dish.

2 Chop or process meats, separately, until coarsely minced; combine in large bowl with remaining ingredients.

3 Press meat mixture into dish; cover with foil. Place terrine dish in baking dish; pour enough boiling water into baking dish to come halfway up side of terrine dish. Cook 1 hour. Uncover; cook a further 1 hour.

4 Remove terrine dish from baking dish; cover terrine with baking paper. Weight with another dish filled with heavy cans; cool 10 minutes then refrigerate overnight.

5 Turn terrine onto serving plate. Serve sliced terrine, at room temperature, with french bread and cornichons, if you like.

nutritional count per serving 28.6g total fat (9.6g saturated fat); 1839kJ (440 cal); 2.5g carbohydrate; 40.4g protein; 0.3g fibre

"Country-style terrine" is the literal meaning
of this classic dish as it is chunky and rustic.
Juniper berries, the dried fruit from the
evergreen tree of the same name, can be found
in specialty spice stores and better delicatessens.

artichoke hearts vinaigrette

prep + cook time 1 hour 30 minutes (+ cooling) **serves** 4

1 medium lemon (140g), chopped coarsely
20 small globe artichokes (2kg)
2 cups (500ml) dry white wine
¼ cup loosely packed fresh thyme leaves
5 cloves garlic, unpeeled
½ cup (125ml) lemon juice
2 teaspoons sea salt flakes
1 cup (250ml) white wine vinegar
2 cups (500ml) water
1 tablespoon extra virgin olive oil

1 Place lemon in large bowl half-filled with water. Discard outer leaves from artichokes; cut tips from remaining leaves. Trim, then peel stalks; place artichokes in lemon water.

2 Cut a piece of baking paper into a round to fit inside a large saucepan.

3 Combine wine, thyme, garlic, juice, salt, vinegar, the water and drained artichokes in large saucepan; cover with baking-paper round. Bring to the boil then simmer, covered, about 25 minutes or until artichokes are tender. Cool in poaching liquid about 30 minutes.

4 Whisk ½ cup of the poaching liquid in small bowl with oil (discard remaining liquid).

5 Halve artichokes lengthwise; using small knife, remove chokes. Divide artichokes among serving bowls; drizzle with poaching mixture. If you like, sprinkle with extra thyme leaves and serve with crusty bread.

—◦◦◦—

nutritional count per serving 5.5g total fat (0.7g saturated fat); 865kJ (207 cal); 6.7g carbohydrate; 10.4g protein; 4.4g fibre

asparagus hollandaise

prep + cook time 35 minutes **serves** 4

1kg asparagus, trimmed
hollandaise sauce
2 tablespoons water
2 tablespoons white wine vinegar
¼ teaspoon cracked black pepper
2 egg yolks
200g unsalted butter, melted

1 Make hollandaise sauce.

2 Boil, steam or microwave asparagus until tender. Serve asparagus on a large platter drizzled with hollandaise sauce.

hollandaise sauce Combine the water, vinegar and pepper in small saucepan; bring to the boil. Reduce heat; simmer, uncovered, until liquid is reduced to 1 tablespoon. Strain mixture through fine sieve into medium heatproof bowl; cool 10 minutes. Whisk egg yolks into vinegar mixture. Set bowl over medium saucepan of simmering water; do not allow water to touch base of bowl. Whisk mixture over heat until thickened. Remove bowl from heat; gradually whisk in melted butter in a thin, steady stream, whisking constantly until sauce is thick and creamy.

nutritional count per serving 44g total fat (26.9g saturated fat); 1797kJ (430 cal); 2.8g carbohydrate; 6.1g protein; 2.6g fibre

garlic prawns

prep + cook time 45 minutes (+ cooling) **serves** 4

1¼ cups (310ml) olive oil

¾ cup (180ml) dry white wine

2 tablespoons lemon juice

6 cloves garlic, sliced thinly

1 fresh long red chilli, chopped finely

1kg uncooked large king prawns

⅓ cup coarsely chopped fresh flat-leaf parsley

1 Preheat oven to 220°C/200°C fan-forced.

2 Combine oil, wine, juice, garlic and chilli in large flameproof baking dish; stir over low heat 5 minutes or until fragrant. Cool 15 minutes.

3 Meanwhile, shell and devein prawns, leaving tails intact.

4 Add prawns to oil mixture; mix well. Transfer to oven; cook 10 minutes or until prawns change colour. Spoon prawn mixture in shallow bowls; sprinkle with parsley. Serve with crusty bread to soak up the juices, if you like.

nutritional count per serving 71.4g total fat (10.1g saturated fat); 3227kJ (772 cal); 0.9g carbohydrate; 26.2g protein; 1g fibre

melon in prosciutto

prep time 20 minutes **serves** 4

1 small rockmelon (1.3kg), halved lengthways

12 thin slices prosciutto (180g)

2 tablespoons extra virgin olive oil

¼ cup loosely packed fresh flat-leaf parsley leaves

1 Peel and seed rockmelon; cut into 12 wedges.

2 Wrap one prosciutto slice around each melon wedge, place on serving platter; drizzle with oil, sprinkle with parsley.

nutritional count per serving 11.9g total fat (2.2g saturated fat); 802kJ (192 cal); 10.9g carbohydrate; 9.4g protein; 2.5g fibre

Classic
Soups

vichyssoise

prep + cook time 45 minutes (+ refrigeration) serves 4

30g butter

1 large brown onion (200g), chopped finely

1 large leek (500g), sliced thickly

4 medium potatoes (800g), chopped coarsely

1.5 litres (6 cups) chicken stock

300ml cream

2 tablespoons finely chopped fresh chives

Vichyssoise (pronounced vish-ee-swaz) is a French-style cold soup made with potatoes and leeks. The origins of whether it is a French dish or an American innovation, is a subject of debate; however, credit for the dish usually goes to Louis Diat, a chef at the Ritz-Carlton in New York City, who claimed he developed the dish in 1917.

1 Heat butter in large saucepan; cook onion and leek, stirring, about 10 minutes or until soft. Add potato and stock; bring to the boil. Reduce heat; simmer, covered, 15 minutes.

2 Blend or process soup, in batches. Stir cream into soup; cover, refrigerate 3 hours or overnight.

3 Serve soup sprinkled with chives.

nutritional count per serving 40.6g total fat (26.3g saturated fat); 2299kJ (550 cal); 32.8g carbohydrate; 12g protein; 5.6g fibre

cream of chicken soup

prep + cook time 3 hours **serves** 4

2 litres (8 cups) water

1 litre (4 cups) chicken stock

1.8kg whole chicken

1 medium carrot (120g), chopped coarsely

1 stalk celery (150g), trimmed, chopped coarsely

1 medium brown onion (150g), chopped coarsely

40g butter

⅓ cup (50g) plain flour

2 tablespoons lemon juice

½ cup (125ml) cream

¼ cup finely chopped fresh flat-leaf parsley

1 Place the water and stock in large saucepan with chicken, carrot, celery and onion; bring to the boil. Reduce heat; simmer, covered, 1½ hours. Remove chicken from pan; simmer broth, covered, 30 minutes.

2 Strain broth through muslin-lined sieve or colander into large heatproof bowl; discard solids.

3 Melt butter in large saucepan, add flour; cook, stirring, until mixture thickens and bubbles. Gradually stir in broth and juice; stir over heat until mixture boils and thickens slightly. Add cream, reduce heat; simmer, uncovered, about 25 minutes, stirring occasionally.

4 Meanwhile, remove and discard skin and bones from chicken; shred meat coarsely. Add chicken to soup; stir over medium heat until hot.

5 Sprinkle soup with parsley; serve with crusty bread, if you like.

nutritional count per serving 59.2g total fat (26.2g saturated fat); 3327kJ (796 cal); 15.7g carbohydrate; 50.7g protein; 2.5g fibre

scotch broth

prep + cook time 2 hours 15 minutes serves 4

2.25 litres (9 cups) water

1kg lamb neck chops

¾ cup (150g) pearl barley

1 large brown onion (200g), chopped coarsely

2 medium carrots (240g), chopped coarsely

1 medium leek (350g), sliced thinly

2 cups (160g) finely shredded savoy cabbage

½ cup (60g) frozen peas

2 tablespoons finely chopped fresh flat-leaf parsley

1 Combine the water in large saucepan with lamb and barley; bring to the boil. Reduce heat; simmer, covered, 1 hour, skimming fat from surface occasionally. Add onion, carrot and leek; simmer, covered, about 30 minutes or until carrot is tender.

2 Remove lamb from pan. When cool enough to handle, remove and discard bones; shred lamb meat coarsely.

3 Return lamb to soup with cabbage and peas; cook, uncovered, about 10 minutes or until peas are tender.

4 Serve soup sprinkled with parsley.

nutritional count per serving 24.4g total fat (10.7g saturated fat); 2274kJ (544 cal); 32.8g carbohydrate; 43.2g protein; 10.7g fibre

minestrone

prep + cook time 4 hours (+ refrigeration) **serves** 6

1 ham hock (1kg)

1 medium brown onion (150g), quartered

1 stalk celery (150g), trimmed, chopped coarsely

1 teaspoon black peppercorns

1 bay leaf

4 litres (16 cups) water

1 tablespoon olive oil

1 large carrot (180g), chopped finely

2 stalks celery (200g), trimmed, chopped finely, extra

3 cloves garlic, crushed

¼ cup (70g) tomato paste

2 large tomatoes (440g), chopped finely

1 small leek (200g), sliced thinly

1 cup (100g) small pasta shells

420g can white beans, rinsed, drained

½ cup coarsely chopped fresh flat-leaf parsley

½ cup coarsely chopped fresh basil

½ cup (40g) flaked parmesan cheese

1 Preheat oven to 220°C/200°C fan-forced.

2 Roast ham hock and onion in baking dish, uncovered, 30 minutes.

3 Combine hock and onion with celery, peppercorns, bay leaf and the water in large saucepan; bring to the boil. Reduce heat; simmer, uncovered, 2 hours.

4 Remove hock from broth. Strain broth through muslin-lined sieve or colander into large heatproof bowl; discard solids. Allow broth to cool, cover; refrigerate until cold.

5 Remove ham from hock; shred coarsely. Discard bone, fat and skin.

6 Meanwhile, heat oil in large saucepan; cook carrot and extra celery, stirring, 2 minutes. Add ham, garlic, paste and tomato; cook, stirring, 2 minutes.

7 Discard fat from surface of broth. Pour broth into a large measuring jug; add enough water to make 2 litres (8 cups). Add broth to pan; bring to the boil. Reduce heat; simmer, covered, 20 minutes.

8 Add leek, pasta and beans to pan; bring to the boil. Reduce heat; simmer, uncovered, until pasta is tender. Remove from heat; stir in herbs. Serve soup sprinkled with cheese.

nutritional count per serving 7.2g total fat (2.4g saturated fat); 865kJ (207 cal); 19.6g carbohydrate; 12.7g protein; 6.1g fibre

fish chowder

prep + cook time 45 minutes **serves** 4

40g butter

1 large brown onion (200g), chopped coarsely

1 clove garlic, crushed

2 rindless bacon rashers (130g), chopped coarsely

2 tablespoons plain flour

2 medium potatoes (400g), chopped coarsely

3 cups (750ml) milk

2 cups (500ml) vegetable stock

400g firm white fish fillets, chopped coarsely

2 tablespoons finely chopped fresh chives

1 Melt butter in large saucepan; cook onion, garlic and bacon, stirring, until onion softens.

2 Add flour to pan; cook, stirring, 1 minute. Add potato, milk and stock; bring to the boil. Reduce heat; simmer, covered, about 10 minutes or until potato is tender.

3 Add fish; simmer, uncovered, about 4 minutes or until fish is barely cooked. Sprinkle soup with chives; serve wtih crusy bread, if you like.

nutritional count per serving 19.5g total fat (11.6g saturated fat); 1810kJ (433 cal); 28.4g carbohydrate; 34.8g protein; 2.4g fibre

borscht

prep time 1 hour 40 minutes **serves** 6

50g butter

2 medium brown onions (300g), chopped coarsely

2kg beetroot, peeled, grated coarsely

2 medium potatoes (400g), chopped coarsely

2 large tomatoes (440g), chopped coarsely

2 medium carrots (240g), chopped coarsely

2.5 litres (10 cups) water

⅓ cup (80ml) red wine vinegar

500g piece gravy beef

3 bay leaves

4 cups (320g) shredded savoy cabbage

½ cup (120g) sour cream

2 tablespoons coarsely chopped fresh flat-leaf parsley

1 Melt butter in large saucepan, add onion; cook, stirring, until soft. Add beetroot, potato, tomato, carrot, the water, vinegar, beef and bay leaves. Bring to the boil; reduce heat, simmer, covered, 1 hour.

2 Remove and discard fat from surface of soup. Remove beef from soup; shred meat using two forks. Return meat to soup with cabbage; simmer, uncovered, 20 minutes.

3 Remove and discard bay leaves. Serve soup topped with sour cream and parsley.

nutritional count per serving 19.1g total fat (11.3g saturated fat); 1952kJ (467 cal); 39.8g carbohydrate; 26.9g protein; 14.6g fibre

french onion soup with gruyère croûtons

prep + cook time 1 hour 10 minutes **serves** 4

50g butter

4 large brown onions (800g), sliced thinly

¾ cup (180ml) dry white wine

3 cups (750ml) water

1 litre (4 cups) beef stock

1 bay leaf

1 tablespoon plain flour

1 teaspoon fresh thyme leaves

gruyère croûtons

1 small french bread (150g), cut in 1.5cm slices

½ cup (60g) coarsely grated gruyère cheese

1 Melt butter in large saucepan, add onion; cook, stirring occasionally, about 30 minutes or until caramelised.

2 Meanwhile, bring wine to the boil in large saucepan; boil 1 minute then stir in the water, stock and bay leaf; return to the boil. Remove from heat.

3 Stir flour into onion mixture; cook, stirring, 2 minutes. Gradually add hot broth mixture to onion mixture, stirring, until mixture boils and thickens slightly. Reduce heat; simmer, uncovered, stirring occasionally, 20 minutes. Discard bay leaf; stir in thyme.

4 Meanwhile, make gruyère croûtons.

5 Serve bowls of soup topped with croûtons. Sprinkle with extra thyme leaves, if you like.

gruyère croûtons Preheat grill. Toast bread on one side then turn and sprinkle with cheese; grill croûtons until cheese browns lightly.

nutritional count per serving 16.7g total fat (10g saturated fat); 1522kJ (364 cal); 31.1g carbohydrate; 13.4g protein; 3.9g fibre

gazpacho

prep time 25 minutes (+ refrigeration) **serves** 4

3 cups (750ml) tomato juice

8 medium egg tomatoes (600g), chopped coarsely

1 medium red onion (170g), chopped coarsely

1 clove garlic

1 lebanese cucumber (130g), chopped coarsely

1 small green capsicum (150g), chopped coarsely

2 slices white bread, crusts removed, chopped coarsely

2 teaspoons Tabasco sauce

1 small white onion (80g), chopped finely

½ lebanese cucumber (65g), seeded, chopped finely

½ small yellow capsicum (75g), chopped finely

2 teaspoons olive oil

1 tablespoon vodka

2 tablespoons finely chopped fresh coriander

1 Blend or process juice, tomato, red onion, garlic, coarsely chopped cucumber, green capsicum, bread and sauce, in batches, until puréed. Strain through sieve into large bowl, cover; refrigerate 3 hours.

2 Combine white onion, finely chopped cucumber, yellow capsicum, oil, vodka and coriander in small bowl.

3 Serve soup topped with vegetable mixture. Serve with crusty bread, if you like.

nutritional count per serving 2.6g total fat (0.3g saturated fat); 548kJ (131 cal); 16.9g carbohydrate; 4.8g protein; 4.9g fibre

The term gazpacho describes a chilled soup that originated in Spain. It is based on a combination of stale bread, garlic, oil and vinegar; later tomato and capsicum were added, and it is this variation that we are most familiar with.

pea and ham soup

prep + cook time 2 hours 15 minutes **serves** 6

1 medium brown onion (150g), chopped coarsely

2 stalks celery (300g), trimmed, chopped coarsely

2 bay leaves

1.5kg ham hocks

2.5 litres (10 cups) water

1 teaspoon cracked black pepper

2 cups (375g) split green peas

1 Combine onion, celery, bay leaves, hocks, the water and pepper in large saucepan; bring to the boil. Reduce heat; simmer, covered, about 1½ hours. Add peas; simmer, covered, 30 minutes or until peas are tender.

2 Remove hocks from pan; when cool enough to handle, remove meat from hocks. Shred meat finely. Discard bones, fat and skin; remove and discard bay leaves.

3 Blend or process half the soup mixture, in batches, until smooth. Return to pan with remaining soup mixture and ham; stir soup until heated through.

nutritional count per serving 4.9g total fat (1.4g saturated fat); 1162kJ (278 cal); 31g carbohydrate; 23.5g protein; 7.3g fibre

Split peas do not need to be soaked in water overnight. The relatively short cooking time produces a soup with more texture than usual.

bouillabaisse with rouille

prep + cook time 1 hour 40 minutes **serves** 6

700g uncooked large prawns

2 uncooked medium blue swimmer crabs (650g)

10 small tomatoes (900g)

1 tablespoon olive oil

1 clove garlic, crushed

1 large brown onion (200g), chopped coarsely

1 medium leek (350g), chopped coarsely

1 baby fennel bulb (130g), chopped coarsely

1 fresh small red thai chilli, chopped coarsely

1 bay leaf

pinch saffron threads

10cm strip fresh orange peel

1.5 litres (6 cups) water

1 cup (250ml) dry white wine

750g firm white fish fillets, chopped coarsely

500g small black mussels

½ cup coarsely chopped fresh flat-leaf parsley

1 small french bread (150g)

rouille

1 medium red capsicum (200g)

1 fresh small red thai chilli, chopped coarsely

1 clove garlic, quartered

1 cup (70g) stale breadcrumbs

1 tablespoon lemon juice

¼ cup (60ml) olive oil

1 Shell and devein prawns, leaving tails intact. Reserve heads and shells; place prawn meat in medium bowl.

2 Slide a knife under top of crab shell at back, lever off shell; reserve with prawn shells. Discard gills; rinse crabs under cold water. Cut crab bodies into quarters; place in bowl with prawn meat.

3 Chop four of the tomatoes coarsely; reserve with seafood shells. Peel remaining tomatoes; remove seeds. Chop flesh finely.

4 Heat oil in large saucepan; cook reserved seafood shell mixture, garlic, onion, leek, fennel, chilli, bay leaf, saffron and peel, stirring, about 10 minutes or until shells change colour and vegetables soften. Add the water and wine, cover; bring to the boil. Reduce heat; simmer, covered, 10 minutes. Remove and discard crab shells.

5 Blend or process seafood mixture (including prawn shells), in batches, until smooth; using a wooden spoon, push each batch through a large sieve into large saucepan. Discard solids in sieve. Reserve ¼ cup strained seafood mixture for rouille.

6 Make rouille.

7 Add finely chopped tomatoes to strained liquid; bring to the boil. Add fish and mussels, return to the boil; cook, covered, 5 minutes. Add reserved prawn meat and crab pieces; cook, covered, 5 minutes. Stir parsley into soup.

8 Preheat grill. Cut bread into slices; toast under grill until browned lightly. Serve soup with toast and rouille.

rouille Quarter capsicum; discard seeds and membrane. Roast under preheated grill or in very hot oven, skin-side up, until skin blisters and blackens. Cover capsicum pieces with plastic or paper for 5 minutes then peel away skin; chop coarsely. Blend or process capsicum with chilli, garlic, breadcrumbs, juice and reserved strained seafood mixture liquid until smooth. With motor operating, gradually add oil in a thin, steady stream; process until rouille thickens.

nutritional count per serving 17.3g total fat (2.9g saturated fat); 2132kJ (510 cal); 29.5g carbohydrate; 48.9g protein; 6.2g fibre

French for "rust", rouille is a capsicum- and chilli-flavoured mayonnaise-like sauce often used to garnish seafood stews. Discard any mussels that do not open.

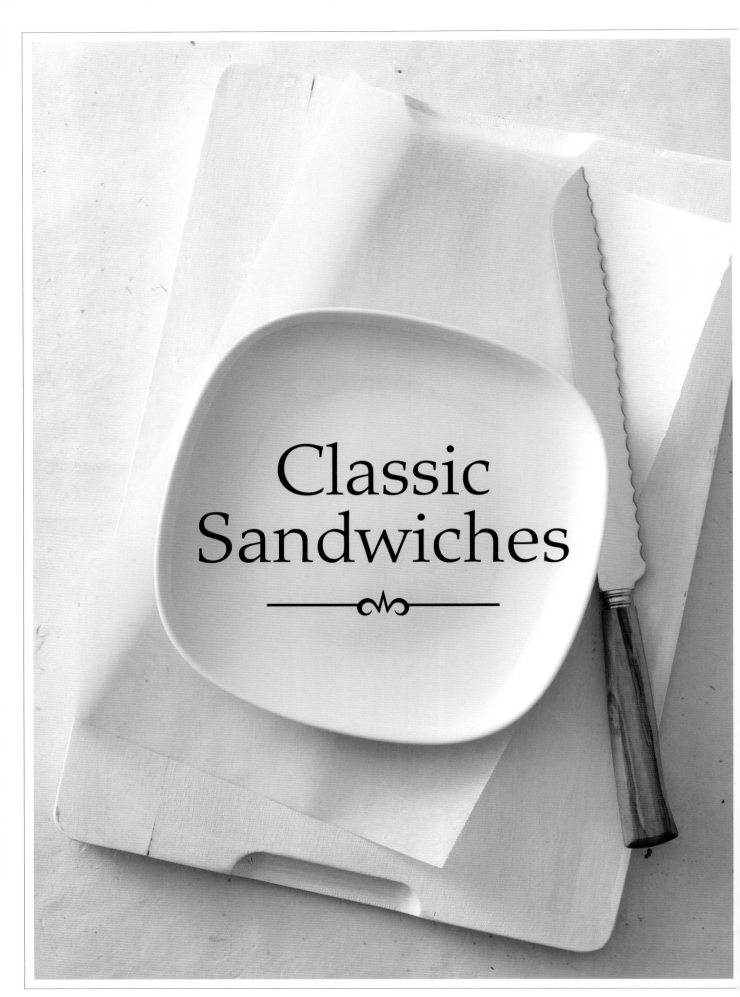

Classic
Sandwiches

club sandwich

prep + cook time 20 minutes **makes** 4

4 rindless bacon rashers (260g), halved

1 medium avocado (250g)

2 teaspoons lime juice

½ cup (150g) mayonnaise

12 slices white bread (540g)

12 large butter lettuce leaves

3 small tomatoes (270g), sliced thinly

150g shaved turkey breast

1 Cook bacon in heated oiled large frying pan until crisp.

2 Mash avocado and juice in small bowl until smooth.

3 Spread mayonnaise over bread slices; top four slices with half the avocado mixture, lettuce, tomato, turkey and bacon. Top with four more slices of bread, mayonnaise-side down, spread top with a little more mayonnaise. Repeat layers with remaining fillings and bread. Cut into triangles; use toothpicks or skewers to hold layers in place.

nutritional count per sandwich 36.1g total fat (7.7g saturated fat); 3210kJ (768 cal); 69.9g carbohydrate; 37.7g protein; 6.3g fibre

blt

prep + cook time 15 minutes **makes** 4

8 rindless bacon rashers (520g)

⅓ cup (100g) mayonnaise

8 thick slices white bread (560g)

8 large butter lettuce leaves

2 small tomatoes (180g), sliced thinly

1 Cook bacon in heated oiled large frying pan until crisp.

2 Spread mayonnaise over half the bread slices; top with lettuce, tomato and bacon. Top with remaining bread.

nutritional count per blt 29.1g total fat (7.8g saturated fat); 2934kJ (702 cal); 69.2g carbohydrate; 37.8g protein; 5.2g fibre

We used slices of white sourdough bread in this recipe.

cucumber sandwiches

prep time 15 minutes **makes** 24

1 telegraph cucumber (400g)
sea salt flakes
16 slices white bread (720g)
50g butter, softened

1 Peel and seed cucumber; slice as thinly as possible. Place cucumber in a strainer or colander, sprinkle with salt. Stand 20 minutes, then rinse cucumber with cold water; drain well. Pat dry with absorbent paper.

2 Spread bread with butter. Sandwich cucumber slices between bread slices.

3 Cut crusts from bread; cut each sandwich into 3 fingers.

nutritional count per finger 2.4g total fat (1.2g saturated fat); 376kJ (90 cal); 13.7g carbohydrate; 3.7g protein; 1g fibre

steak sandwich

prep + cook time 30 minutes **makes** 4

2 cloves garlic, crushed

2 tablespoons olive oil

4 thin beef scotch fillet steaks (500g)

2 medium brown onions (200g), sliced thinly

1 tablespoon brown sugar

1 tablespoon balsamic vinegar

8 thick slices white bread (560g)

1 baby cos lettuce (180g), leaves separated

2 dill pickles (40g) sliced thinly

¼ cup (80g) tomato chutney

1 Combine garlic and half the oil in medium bowl; add steaks, rub both sides with mixture.

2 Heat remaining oil in medium frying pan; cook onion over low heat, stirring occasionally, about 10 minutes or until soft. Add sugar and vinegar; cook, stirring, about 5 minutes or until caramelised. Remove from pan.

3 Meanwhile, cook steaks in heated oiled large frying pan.

4 Toast bread both sides. Sandwich lettuce, steaks, onion, pickle and chutney between toast slices.

nutritional count per sandwich 20.5g total fat (5g saturated fat); 2809kJ (672 cal); 78.1g carbohydrate; 39.7g protein; 6.4g fibre

We used slices of white sourdough bread in this recipe.

curried egg sandwiches

prep time 15 minutes **makes** 16

6 hard-boiled eggs, chopped coarsely

⅓ cup (100g) mayonnaise

2 teaspoons curry powder

8 slices white bread (360g)

2 cups shredded iceberg lettuce

1 Use a fork to mash egg, mayonnaise and curry powder in medium bowl.

2 Sandwich egg mixture then lettuce between bread slices. Cut crusts from bread; cut each sandwich into four triangles to serve.

nutritional count per triangle 4.6g total fat (1g saturated fat); 448kJ (107 cal); 11.5g carbohydrate; 4.5g protein; 0.9g fibre

chicken, mayo, celery and walnut fingers

prep time 40 minutes **makes** 30

3 cups (480g) finely chopped cooked chicken
4 green onions, chopped finely
½ cup (60g) finely chopped roasted walnuts
3 stalks celery (450g), trimmed, chopped finely
½ cup (150g) mayonnaise
⅓ cup (80g) sour cream
20 slices white bread (900g)
10 slices wholemeal bread (450g)

1 Combine chicken, onion, nuts, celery, mayonnaise and sour cream in large bowl.
2 Spread 2 tablespoons of the chicken mixture onto half the white bread; top each with a slice of brown bread. Spread another 2 tablespoons of chicken mixture over top of brown bread then top with remaining white bread.
3 Remove crusts; cut each sandwich into three fingers.

nutritional count per finger 6.6g total fat
(1.5g saturated fat); 752kJ (180 cal);
20.4g carbohydrate; 8.5g protein; 2.1g fibre

tuna salad sandwiches

prep time 15 minutes **makes** 16

425g can tuna in brine, drained, flaked
½ small red capsicum (75g), chopped finely
1 green onion, sliced thinly
1 stalk celery (150g), trimmed, chopped finely
1 teaspoon finely chopped fresh flat-leaf parsley
½ cup (150g) mayonnaise
2 teaspoons lemon juice
1 teaspoon dijon mustard
8 slices multigrain bread (360g)
90g green oak lettuce leaves

1 Combine tuna, capsicum, onion, celery and parsley in medium bowl. Stir in the combined mayonnaise, juice and mustard.
2 Spread a quarter of the tuna mixture over four bread slices; top with lettuce then remaining bread. Cut into triangles to serve.

nutritional count per triangle 4.2g total fat (0.6g saturated fat); 487kJ (116 cal); 11.7g carbohydrate; 7.2g protein; 1.7g fibre

croque-monsieur

prep + cook time 30 minutes **makes** 4

8 slices wholemeal bread (360g)
8 slices leg ham (180g)
40g butter
cheese sauce
20g butter
1 tablespoon plain flour
¾ cup (180ml) milk
¾ cup (90g) coarsely grated cheddar cheese
1 tablespoon finely chopped fresh flat-leaf parsley

1 Make cheese sauce.
2 Spread sauce over bread slices; top four slices with ham then top with remaining bread.
3 Melt butter in large frying pan. Add sandwiches; cook, in batches, until browned both sides. Cut into triangles to serve.
cheese sauce Melt butter in small saucepan, add flour; cook, stirring, until mixture bubbles and thickens. Gradually add milk; cook, stirring, until sauce boils and thickens. Remove from heat; stir in cheese and parsley.

nutritional count per sandwich 25.9g total fat (15g saturated fat); 2077kJ (497 cal); 38.4g carbohydrate; 24.8g protein; 5.8g fibre

A croque-monsieur is a pan-fried ham and cheese sandwich.
It originated in France in the early 1900s. The name is based
on the words croquer (to crunch) and monsieur (mister).

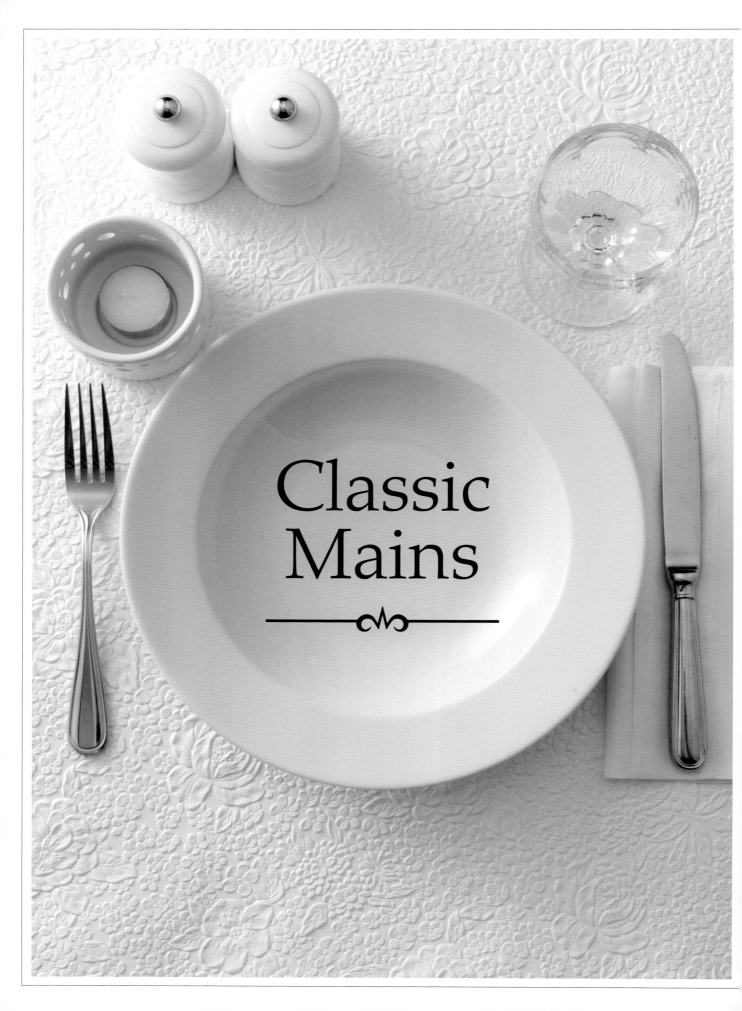

Classic
Mains

boeuf bourguignon

prep + cook time 2 hours 45 minutes **serves** 6

300g baby brown onions

2 tablespoons olive oil

2kg gravy beef, trimmed, chopped coarsely

30g butter

4 rindless bacon rashers (260g), chopped coarsely

400g button mushrooms, halved

2 cloves garlic, crushed

¼ cup (35g) plain flour

1¼ cups (310ml) beef stock

2½ cups (625ml) dry red wine

2 bay leaves

2 sprigs fresh thyme

½ cup coarsely chopped fresh flat-leaf parsley

1 Peel onions, leaving root end intact so onion remains whole during cooking.

2 Heat oil in large flameproof dish; cook beef, in batches, until browned.

3 Add butter to dish; cook onions, bacon, mushrooms and garlic, stirring, until onions are browned lightly.

4 Sprinkle flour over onion mixture; cook, stirring, until flour mixture thickens and bubbles. Gradually add stock and wine; stir over heat until mixture boils and thickens. Return beef and any juices to dish, add bay leaves and thyme; bring to the boil. Reduce heat; simmer, covered, about 2 hours or until beef is tender, stirring every 30 minutes.

5 Remove from heat; discard bay leaves. Stir in parsley.

nutritional count per serving 31.4g total fat (12.1g saturated fat); 2658kJ (636 cal); 6.6g carbohydrate; 80.3g protein; 2.8g fibre

pastitsio

prep + cook time 2 hours 15 minutes **serves** 6

250g macaroni pasta

2 eggs, beaten lightly

¾ cup (60g) coarsely grated parmesan cheese

2 tablespoons stale breadcrumbs

meat sauce

2 tablespoons olive oil

2 medium brown onions (300g), chopped finely

750g beef mince

400g can crushed tomatoes

⅓ cup (90g) tomato paste

½ cup (125ml) beef stock

¼ cup (60ml) dry white wine

½ teaspoon ground cinnamon

1 egg, beaten lightly

cheese topping

90g butter

½ cup (75g) plain flour

3½ cups (875ml) milk

1 cup (80g) coarsely grated parmesan cheese

2 egg yolks

1 Preheat oven to 180°C/160°C fan-forced. Oil shallow 2.5-litre (10-cup) ovenproof dish.

2 Make meat sauce; make cheese topping.

3 Cook pasta in large saucepan of boiling water until tender; drain. Combine hot pasta, egg and cheese in large bowl. Press pasta over base of dish.

4 Top pasta evenly with meat sauce; pour over cheese topping. Smooth surface; sprinkle with breadcrumbs. Bake, in oven, about 1 hour or until browned lightly. Stand 10 minutes before serving.

meat sauce Heat oil in large saucepan, add onion and beef; cook, stirring, until beef is browned. Stir in undrained tomatoes, paste, stock, wine and cinnamon; simmer, uncovered, about 20 minutes or until mixture is thick. Cool; stir in egg.

cheese topping Melt butter in medium saucepan, add flour; cook, stirring, until mixture bubbles and thickens. Remove from heat; gradually stir in milk. Stir over heat until sauce boils and thickens; stir in cheese. Cool 5 minutes; stir in egg yolks.

nutritional count per serving 45.8g total fat (22.7g saturated fat); 3528kJ (844 cal); 52.5g carbohydrate; 52.1g protein; 4.1g fibre

moussaka

prep + cook time 1 hour 50 minutes **serves** 6

¼ cup (60ml) olive oil

2 large eggplants (1kg), sliced thinly

1 large brown onion (200g), chopped finely

2 cloves garlic, crushed

1kg lamb mince

425g can crushed tomatoes

½ cup (125ml) dry white wine

1 teaspoon ground cinnamon

¼ cup (20g) finely grated parmesan cheese

white sauce

80g butter

⅓ cup (50g) plain flour

2 cups (500ml) milk

1 Heat oil in large frying pan; cook eggplant, in batches, until browned both sides; drain on absorbent paper.

2 Cook onion and garlic in same pan, stirring, until onion softens. Add mince; cook, stirring, until mince changes colour. Stir in undrained tomatoes, wine and cinnamon; bring to the boil. Reduce heat; simmer, uncovered, about 30 minutes or until liquid has evaporated.

3 Meanwhile, preheat oven to 180°C/160°C fan-forced. Oil shallow 2-litre (8-cup) rectangular baking dish.

4 Make white sauce.

5 Place a third of the eggplant, overlapping slices slightly, in dish; spread half the meat sauce over eggplant. Repeat layering with another third of the eggplant, remaining meat sauce and remaining eggplant. Spread white sauce over top layer of eggplant; sprinkle with cheese.

6 Bake moussaka about 40 minutes or until top browns lightly. Cover; stand 10 minutes before serving. Serve with a green salad, if you like.

white sauce Melt butter in medium saucepan. Add flour; cook, stirring, until mixture bubbles and thickens. Gradually add milk; stir until mixture boils and thickens.

nutritional count per serving 36.6g total fat (16.5g saturated fat); 2420kJ (579 cal); 18g carbohydrate; 41.8g protein; 5.3g fibre

fettuccine carbonara

prep + cook time 20 minutes **serves** 4

500g fresh fettuccine pasta

60g butter

6 rindless bacon rashers (390g), sliced thinly

1 clove garlic, crushed

½ teaspoon cracked black pepper

300ml cream

2 eggs, beaten lightly

½ cup (40g) finely grated parmesan cheese

½ cup (40g) finely grated romano cheese

2 teaspoons coarsely chopped fresh chives

1 Cook pasta in large saucepan of boiling water until tender; drain.

2 Meanwhile, melt butter in medium frying pan; cook bacon, stirring, 5 minutes.

3 Add garlic, pepper and cream to pan; simmer, uncovered, until sauce reduces by half. Remove from heat. Stir in egg and cheeses.

4 Add pasta to sauce; stir to coat. Serve pasta sprinkled with chives.

nutritional count per serving 66.7g total fat (39g saturated fat); 3662kJ (876 cal); 33.6g carbohydrate; 53.7g protein; 2.4g fibre

macaroni cheese

prep + cook time 1 hour **serves** 4

300g macaroni pasta

4 rindless bacon rashers (260g), chopped finely

50g butter

⅓ cup (50g) plain flour

1 litre (4 cups) milk

1 cup (120g) coarsely grated cheddar cheese

½ cup (40g) finely grated pecorino cheese

2 tablespoons wholegrain mustard

½ cup (35g) stale breadcrumbs

20g butter, extra

1 Preheat oven to 180°C/160°C fan-forced. Oil deep 2-litre (8-cup) ovenproof dish.

2 Cook pasta in large saucepan of boiling water until tender; drain.

3 Meanwhile, cook bacon in medium saucepan, stirring, until crisp; drain on absorbent paper.

4 Melt butter in same pan, add flour; cook, stirring, 1 minute. Gradually stir in milk; cook, stirring, until sauce boils and thickens. Cool 2 minutes; stir in cheeses and mustard.

5 Combine pasta, sauce and bacon in large bowl; pour mixture into ovenproof dish. Top with breadcrumbs, dot with extra butter. Bake, in oven, about 30 minutes or until browned.

nutritional count per serving 47.5g total fat (27.8g saturated fat); 3854kJ (922 cal); 78.8g carbohydrate; 43.1g protein; 3.5g fibre

quiche lorraine

prep + cook time 1 hour 30 minutes (+ refrigeration) **serves** 6

1 medium brown onion (150g), chopped finely

3 rindless bacon rashers (195g), chopped finely

3 eggs

300ml cream

½ cup (125ml) milk

¾ cup (120g) coarsely grated gruyère cheese

pastry

1¾ cups (260g) plain flour

150g cold butter, chopped coarsely

1 egg yolk

2 teaspoons lemon juice

⅓ cup (80ml) iced water, approximately

1 Make pastry.

2 Preheat oven to 200°C/180°C fan-forced.

3 Roll pastry between sheets of baking paper large enough to line a deep 23cm loose-based flan tin. Lift pastry into tin; gently press pastry around side. Trim edge, place tin on oven tray. Cover pastry with baking paper; fill with dried beans or rice. Bake 10 minutes; remove paper and beans. Bake pastry a further 10 minutes or until golden brown; cool.

4 Reduce oven temperature to 180°C/160°C fan-forced.

5 Cook onion and bacon in heated oiled small frying pan until onion is soft; drain on absorbent paper, cool. Sprinkle bacon mixture over pastry case.

6 Whisk eggs in medium bowl then whisk in cream, milk and cheese; pour into pastry case. Bake, in oven, about 35 minutes or until filling is set. Stand 5 minutes before removing quiche from tin.

pastry Sift flour into bowl; rub in butter. Add egg yolk, juice and enough water to make ingredients cling together. Knead gently on lightly floured surface until smooth; cover, refrigerate 30 minutes.

nutritional count per serving 51.8g total fat (35.4g saturated fat); 3139kJ (751 cal); 35.4g carbohydrate; 22.1g protein; 2g fibre

Calasparra rice is a short-grain rice available from Spanish delicatessens and gourmet-food stores. If you can't find calasparra, any short-grain rice can be substituted.

paella

prep + cook time 2 hours (+ standing) **serves** 6

500g clams

1 tablespoon coarse cooking salt

500g uncooked medium prawns

500g small black mussels

2 tablespoons olive oil

3 cups (750ml) chicken stock

pinch saffron threads

220g chicken thigh fillets, chopped coarsely

1 chorizo sausage (170g), sliced thickly

1 large red onion (300g), chopped finely

1 medium red capsicum (200g), chopped finely

2 cloves garlic, crushed

2 teaspoons smoked paprika

2 medium tomatoes (300g), peeled, seeded, chopped finely

1½ cups (300g) calasparra rice

1 cup (120g) frozen peas

2 tablespoons finely chopped fresh flat-leaf parsley

1 Rinse clams under cold water, place in large bowl with salt; cover with cold water, stand 2 hours. Drain then rinse.

2 Shell and devein prawns, leaving tails intact. Reserve shells. Scrub mussels and remove beards.

3 Heat 2 teaspoons of the oil in large saucepan, add prawn shells; cook, stirring, until red. Add stock; bring to the boil. Reduce heat; simmer, uncovered, 20 minutes. Strain through fine sieve into jug or bowl; add saffron to the liquid. Discard prawn shells.

4 Heat another 2 teaspoons of the oil in 45cm paella pan or large frying pan, add chicken; cook until browned all over, remove from pan. Add chorizo to same pan; cook until browned all over. Remove chorizo from pan; drain on absorbent paper.

5 Heat remaining oil in pan, add onion, capsicum, garlic, paprika and tomato; cook, stirring, until soft. Add rice; stir to coat in mixture.

6 Add chicken, chorizo and stock to pan; stir until combined. Bring mixture to the boil; reduce heat, simmer, uncovered, about 15 minutes or until rice is almost tender.

7 Sprinkle peas over rice; place clams, prawns and mussels evenly over surface of paella. Cover pan with a lid or large sheets of foil; simmer about 5 minutes or until prawns are cooked and mussels and clams have opened (discard any that do not). Sprinkle with parsley; serve immediately.

nutritional count per serving 18.9g total fat (5.2g saturated fat); 2128kJ (509 cal); 49.1g carbohydrate; 33.6g protein; 3.7g fibre

chicken cacciatore

prep + cook time 1 hours 30 minutes **serves** 4

2 tablespoons olive oil

1.5kg chicken thigh cutlets, skin on

1 medium brown onion (150g), chopped finely

1 clove garlic, crushed

½ cup (125ml) dry white wine

2 tablespoons white wine vinegar

½ cup (125ml) chicken stock

410g can crushed tomatoes

¼ cup (70g) tomato paste

2 drained anchovy fillets, chopped finely

½ cup (60g) seeded black olives, chopped coarsely

½ cup coarsely chopped fresh flat-leaf parsley

1 Heat half the oil in large saucepan; cook chicken, in batches, until browned all over.

2 Heat remaining oil in same pan; cook onion and garlic, stirring, until onion softens. Stir in wine, vinegar, stock, undrained tomatoes, paste and anchovies.

3 Return chicken to pan, fitting pieces tightly together in a single layer; bring to the boil. Reduce heat; simmer, covered, 20 minutes. Uncover; simmer about 30 minutes or until chicken is tender and sauce is reduced. Skim fat from surface; stir in olives and parsley.

nutritional count per serving 39.9g total fat (10.8g saturated fat); 2454kJ (587 cal); 10.8g carbohydrate; 40.5g protein; 3.1g fibre

coq au vin

prep + cook time 1 hour 30 minutes **serves** 4

800g spring onions

¼ cup (60ml) olive oil

6 rindless bacon rashers (390g), chopped coarsely

300g button mushrooms

2 cloves garlic, crushed

8 chicken thigh fillets (880g)

¼ cup (35g) plain flour

2 cups (500ml) dry red wine

1½ cups (375ml) chicken stock

2 tablespoons tomato paste

3 bay leaves

4 sprigs fresh thyme

2 sprigs fresh rosemary

1 Trim green ends from onions, leaving about 4cm of stem attached; trim roots. Heat 1 tablespoon of the oil in large frying pan; cook onions, stirring, until browned all over; remove from pan.

2 Add bacon, mushrooms and garlic to pan; cook, stirring, until bacon is crisp, remove from pan.

3 Coat chicken in flour; shake off excess. Heat remaining oil in same pan. Cook chicken, in batches, until browned all over; drain on absorbent paper.

4 Return chicken to pan with wine, stock, paste, bay leaves, herbs, onions and bacon mixture. Bring to the boil; reduce heat, simmer, uncovered, about 35 minutes or until chicken is tender and sauce has thickened slightly.

nutritional count per serving 43.6g total fat (11.8g saturated fat); 3428kJ (820 cal); 16.3g carbohydrate; 67.8g protein; 6.4g fibre

osso buco

prep + cook time 2 hours 45 minutes **serves** 6

12 pieces veal osso buco (3.5kg)

¼ cup (35g) plain flour

¼ cup (60ml) olive oil

40g butter

1 medium brown onion (150g), chopped coarsely

2 cloves garlic, crushed

3 celery stalks (450g), trimmed, chopped coarsely

2 large carrots (360g), chopped coarsely

4 medium tomatoes (600g), chopped coarsely

2 tablespoons tomato paste

1 cup (250ml) dry white wine

1 cup (250ml) beef stock

400g can crushed tomatoes

3 sprigs fresh thyme

¼ cup coarsely chopped fresh flat-leaf parsley

gremolata

1 tablespoon finely grated lemon rind

⅓ cup finely chopped fresh flat-leaf parsley

2 cloves garlic, chopped finely

1 Coat veal in flour, shake off excess.

2 Heat oil in large flameproof dish; cook veal, in batches, until browned all over.

3 Melt butter in same flameproof dish; cook onion, garlic, celery and carrot, stirring, until vegetables soften. Stir in remaining ingredients.

4 Return veal to dish, fitting pieces upright and tightly together in a single layer; bring to the boil. Cover, reduce heat; simmer 1¾ hours. Uncover; cook 30 minutes.

5 Meanwhile, make gremolata.

6 Remove veal from dish; cover to keep warm. Bring sauce to the boil; boil, uncovered, about 10 minutes or until sauce thickens slightly.

7 Divide veal among serving plates; top with sauce, sprinkle with gremolata. Osso buco can be served with mashed potato or soft polenta, if you like.

gremolata Combine ingredients in small bowl.

nutritional count per serving 16.3g total fat (5.2g saturated fat); 2056kJ (492 cal); 14g carbohydrate; 63.2g protein; 6g fibre

This recipe goes well with creamy polenta: combine 2 cups of milk and 2 cups of water in a large saucepan and bring to the boil. Gradually stir in 1 cup of polenta. Reduce the heat and simmer, stirring, about 5 minutes or until the polenta thickens. Stir in ½ cup finely grated parmesan cheese and ⅓ cup hot milk.

Ask your butcher to cut the veal shin into fairly thick (about 4cm) pieces for you. Standing veal pieces upright helps keep the bone marrow intact.

veal parmigiana

prep + cook time 1 hour 45 minutes **serves** 4

4 veal steaks (320g)

¼ cup (35g) plain flour

1 egg

1 tablespoon water

⅓ cup (25g) stale breadcrumbs

30g butter

⅓ cup (80ml) olive oil

1½ cups (150g) coarsely grated mozzarella cheese

⅓ cup (25g) finely grated parmesan cheese

tomato sauce

1 tablespoon olive oil

1 medium brown onion (150g), chopped finely

1 stalk celery (150g), trimmed, chopped finely

1 medium red capsicum (200g), chopped finely

1 clove garlic, crushed

400g can crushed tomatoes

2 teaspoons white sugar

1 tablespoon tomato paste

1½ cups (375ml) chicken stock

1 tablespoon finely chopped fresh flat-leaf parsley

1 tablespoon finely chopped fresh basil

1 Make tomato sauce.

2 Pound veal out thinly between layers of plastic wrap. Coat veal in flour; shake off excess. Dip veal in combined beaten egg and the water; press breadcrumbs firmly onto veal. Refrigerate 10 minutes.

3 Preheat oven to 180°C/160°C fan-forced.

4 Heat butter and half the oil in large frying pan; cook veal, in batches, until browned both sides. Place in large shallow ovenproof dish; top veal with mozzarella, drizzle with tomato sauce then sprinkle evenly with parmesan. Drizzle over remaining oil. Bake, in oven, about 20 minutes or until browned lightly. Serve with a green salad, if you like.

tomato sauce Heat oil in medium frying pan; cook onion, celery, capsicum and garlic, stirring, until onion is soft; remove from heat. Push undrained tomatoes through a sieve into the pan; discard solids. Add sugar, paste and stock. Cover; bring to the boil. Reduce heat; simmer, covered, 30 minutes. Uncover; simmer until sauce is thick. Stir in herbs.

nutritional count per serving 42g total fat (14.8g saturated fat); 2592kJ (620 cal); 21g carbohydrate; 37g protein; 3.7g fibre

veal scaloppine

prep + cook time 30 minutes **serves** 4

8 veal schnitzels (800g)

¼ cup (35g) plain flour

2 tablespoons olive oil

20g butter

2 tablespoons lemon juice

¼ cup (60ml) dry white wine

1 clove garlic, crushed

¾ cup (180ml) chicken stock

2 tablespoons baby capers, rinsed, drained

¼ cup coarsely chopped fresh flat-leaf parsley

1 Coat veal in flour; shake off excess. Heat oil and butter in large frying pan; cook veal, in batches. Cover to keep warm.

2 Add juice, wine and garlic to pan; bring to the boil. Reduce heat; simmer, uncovered, until liquid is reduced by half. Add stock; simmer, uncovered, 5 minutes. Remove from heat; stir in capers and parsley.

3 Serve veal topped with sauce, and accompany with mashed potato and roasted cherry truss tomatoes, if you like.

nutritional count per serving 16.6g total fat (4.9g saturated fat); 1572kJ (376 cal); 7.7g carbohydrate; 46.3g protein; 0.8g fibre

Veal schnitzel is thinly sliced steak available crumbed or plain (uncrumbed); we use plain schnitzel, sometimes called escalopes, in our recipes.

veal saltimbocca

prep + cook time 35 minutes **serves** 4

8 veal schnitzels (800g)

8 slices prosciutto (120g)

16 fresh sage leaves

40g butter

1 cup (250ml) dry white wine

1 tablespoon lemon juice

2 tablespoons coarsely chopped fresh sage

1 Top each piece of veal with prosciutto and sage leaves. Fold in half to secure filling; secure with toothpicks or small skewers.

2 Melt half the butter in large frying pan; cook veal, in batches, until cooked as desired. Cover to keep warm.

3 Add wine to pan; bring to the boil. Boil, uncovered, until reduced by half. Stir in remaining butter, juice and sage.

4 Serve saltimbocca with sauce, and accompany with steamed green beans and baby new potatoes, if you like.

nutritional count per serving 13g total fat (6.8g saturated fat); 1509kJ (361 cal); 0.5g carbohydrate; 50.3g protein; 0g fibre

Veal schnitzel is thinly sliced steak available crumbed or plain (uncrumbed); we use plain schnitzel, sometimes called escalopes, in our recipes.

beef wellington

prep + cook time 1 hour 20 minutes serves 4

1 tablespoon olive oil

800g piece beef fillet

25g butter

1 small brown onion (80g), chopped finely

125g button mushrooms, chopped finely

150g chicken or duck liver pâté

2 sheets ready-rolled puff pastry

1 egg

1 Heat oil in large frying pan; cook beef until browned all over. Wrap in foil; cool.

2 Heat butter in same pan; cook onion and mushrooms, stirring, until tender. Cool.

3 Preheat oven to 240°C/220°C fan-forced. Line oven tray with baking paper.

4 Stir pâté in medium bowl until soft. Spread over top of beef; top with mushroom mixture.

5 Roll out pastry on lightly floured surface into a rectangle large enough to enclose beef; moisten edges with water. Place beef on one end of rectangle, fold pastry over beef; trim excess pastry and press edges to seal. Place beef on tray; brush with egg then cut small slits in top of pastry.

6 Bake beef 10 minutes. Reduce temperature to 200°C/180°C fan-forced; bake a further 20 minutes or until browned lightly. Slice thickly; serve with a leafy green salad, if you like.

nutritional count per serving 52.2g total fat (23g saturated fat); 3449kJ (825 cal); 31.9g carbohydrate; 56.4g protein; 2.7g fibre

spaghetti bolognese

prep + cook time 2 hours 35 minutes **serves** 6

2 teaspoons olive oil

6 slices pancetta (90g), chopped finely

1 large white onion (200g), chopped finely

1 medium carrot (120g), chopped finely

2 celery stalks (300g) trimmed, chopped finely

600g beef mince

150g chicken livers, trimmed, chopped finely

1 cup (250ml) milk

50g butter

1½ cups (375ml) beef stock

1 cup (250ml) dry red wine

410g can tomato purée

2 tablespoons tomato paste

¼ cup finely chopped fresh flat-leaf parsley

750g fresh spaghetti

½ cup (40g) shaved parmesan cheese

1 Heat oil in large heavy-based frying pan; cook pancetta, stirring, until crisp. Add onion, carrot and celery; cook, stirring, until vegetables soften.

2 Add beef and liver to pan; cook, stirring, until beef changes colour. Stir in milk and butter; cook, stirring occasionally, until liquid reduces to about half.

3 Add stock, wine, purée and paste to pan; simmer, covered, 1 hour. Uncover; simmer 1 hour. Remove from heat; stir in parsley.

4 Meanwhile, cook pasta in large saucepan of boiling water until tender; drain.

5 Serve pasta topped with bolognese sauce and cheese.

— ❧ —

nutritional count per serving 26.6g total fat (13g saturated fat); 2504kJ (599 cal); 41g carbohydrate; 39.2g protein; g5.5 fibre

You can substitute 500g dried spaghetti for the fresh spaghetti, if you prefer.

roast beef with yorkshire puddings

prep + cook time 2 hours 35 minutes (+ refrigeration & standing) **serves** 8

2kg corner piece beef topside roast

2 cups (500ml) dry red wine

2 bay leaves

6 black peppercorns

¼ cup (70g) wholegrain mustard

4 cloves garlic, sliced

4 sprigs fresh thyme

1 medium brown onion (150g), chopped coarsely

2 medium carrots (240g), chopped coarsely

1 large leek (500g), chopped coarsely

2 stalks celery (300g), trimmed, chopped coarsely

2 tablespoons olive oil

yorkshire puddings

1 cup (150g) plain flour

2 eggs

½ cup (125ml) milk

½ cup (125ml) water

gravy

2 tablespoons plain flour

1½ cups (375ml) beef stock

1 Combine beef, wine, bay leaves, peppercorns, mustard, garlic, thyme and onion in large bowl, cover; refrigerate 3 hours or overnight.

2 Preheat oven to 180°C/160°C fan-forced.

3 Drain beef over medium bowl; reserve 1 cup (250ml) of marinade. Combine carrot, leek and celery in large baking dish, top with beef; brush beef with oil.

4 Roast beef, uncovered, about 1½ hours. Remove beef from dish, wrap in foil; stand 20 minutes before serving.

5 Increase oven temperature to 220°C/200°C fan-forced.

6 Remove vegetables with slotted spoon; discard vegetables. Pour pan juices into jug; stand 2 minutes. Reserve 1½ tablespoons oil for yorkshire puddings, pour off excess oil; reserve 2 tablespoons of pan juices for gravy.

7 Make yorkshire puddings and gravy. Serve beef with yorkshire puddings and gravy; accompany with roasted potatoes and steamed baby carrots, if you like.

yorkshire puddings Sift flour into medium bowl; whisk in combined eggs, milk and water all at once until smooth. Stand batter 30 minutes. Divide the reserved oil among eight holes of 12-hole (⅓-cup/80ml) muffin pan; heat in oven 2 minutes. Divide batter among pan holes. Bake about 20 minutes or until puddings are puffed and golden.

gravy Heat reserved pan juices in same baking dish, add flour; cook, stirring, until browned. Gradually add stock and reserved marinade; cook, stirring, until mixture boils and thickens. Strain gravy into heatproof jug.

nutritional count per serving 15.4g total fat (4.8g saturated fat); 2169kJ (519 cal); 21.1g carbohydrate; 61.2g protein; 4g fibre

roast chicken with herb stuffing

prep + cook time 2 hours 15 minutes **serves** 4

1.5kg chicken

20g butter, melted

herb stuffing

1½ cups (105g) stale breadcrumbs

1 stalk celery (150g), trimmed, chopped finely

1 small white onion (100g), chopped finely

1 teaspoon dried mixed herbs

1 egg, beaten lightly

50g butter, melted

1 Preheat oven to 200°C/180°C fan-forced.

2 Make herb stuffing. Fill chicken cavity with stuffing, fold over skin to enclose; secure with toothpicks. Tie legs together with kitchen string.

3 Place chicken on rack over baking dish half-filled with water (water should not touch chicken). Brush chicken with melted butter; roast 15 minutes. Reduce oven temperature to 180°C/160°C fan-forced; roast chicken about 1½ hours or until cooked through.

4 Stand chicken 10 minutes before serving. Serve the chicken with steamed asparagus and roasted baby new potatoes, if you like.

herb stuffing Combine ingredients in medium bowl.

nutritional count per serving 46.8g total fat (19.4g saturated fat); 2817kJ (674 cal); 19.7g carbohydrate; 43.4g protein; 1.9g fibre

shepherd's pie

prep + cook time 1 hour serves 4

30g butter

1 medium brown onion (150g), chopped finely

1 medium carrot (120g), chopped finely

½ teaspoon dried mixed herbs

4 cups (750g) finely chopped cooked lamb

¼ cup (70g) tomato paste

¼ cup (60ml) tomato sauce

2 tablespoons worcestershire sauce

2 cups (500ml) beef stock

2 tablespoons plain flour

⅓ cup (80ml) water

potato topping

5 medium potatoes (1kg), chopped coarsely

60g butter

¼ cup (60ml) milk

1 Preheat oven to 200°C/180°C fan-forced. Oil shallow 2.5-litre (10-cup) ovenproof dish.

2 Make potato topping.

3 Meanwhile, heat butter in large saucepan; cook onion and carrot, stirring, until tender. Add mixed herbs and lamb; cook, stirring, 2 minutes. Stir in paste, sauces and stock, then blended flour and water; stir over heat until mixture boils and thickens. Pour mixture into dish.

4 Drop heaped tablespoons of potato topping onto lamb mixture. Bake in oven about 20 minutes or until browned and heated through.

potato topping Boil, steam or microwave potato until tender; drain. Mash with butter and milk until smooth.

nutritional count per serving 36.2g total fat (20.2g saturated fat); 2976kJ (712 cal); 44.7g carbohydrate; 48.8g protein; 6g fibre

meat pies

prep + cook time 1 hour 35 minutes (+ refrigeration) **makes** 6

1½ cups (225g) plain flour

100g cold butter, chopped coarsely

1 egg

1 tablespoon iced water, approximately

2 sheets ready-rolled puff pastry

1 egg, extra

beef filling

1 tablespoon vegetable oil

1 small brown onion (80g), chopped finely

600g beef mince

415g can crushed tomatoes

2 tablespoons tomato paste

2 tablespoons worcestershire sauce

¾ cup (180ml) beef stock

1 Process flour and butter until crumbly. Add egg and enough of the water to make ingredients cling together. Knead pastry on lightly floured surface until smooth. Cover; refrigerate 30 minutes.

2 Meanwhile, make beef filling.

3 Oil six ⅔-cup (160ml) pie tins. Divide pastry into six portions; roll each between sheets of baking paper until large enough to line tins. Lift pastry into tins; gently press over base and sides; trim. Refrigerate 30 minutes.

4 Cut six 11cm rounds from puff pastry. Refrigerate until required.

5 Preheat oven to 200°C/180°C fan-forced.

6 Place pastry cases on oven tray; line pastry with baking paper then fill with dried beans or uncooked rice. Bake 10 minutes; remove paper and beans. Bake a further 5 minutes; cool.

7 Fill pastry cases with beef filling; brush edges of pastry with extra egg. Top with puff pastry rounds; press edges to seal. Brush tops with egg. Cut steam holes in top of pies. Bake about 20 minutes or until pastry is golden. Serve pies with tomato sauce, if you like.

beef filling Heat oil in large saucepan, add onion and beef; cook, stirring, until beef is well browned. Stir in undrained tomatoes, paste, sauce and stock; bring to the boil. Reduce heat, simmer, uncovered, about 20 minutes or until thick. Cool.

nutritional count per pie 38.7g total fat (13.8g saturated fat); 2876kJ (688 cal); 52.4g carbohydrate; 31.2g protein; 3.5g fibre

chicken and leek pie

prep + cook time 1 hour 35 minutes **serves** 6

2 cups (500ml) chicken stock

600g chicken breast fillets

1 tablespoon olive oil

40g butter

1 large leek (500g), sliced thinly

2 stalks celery (300g), trimmed, chopped finely

2 tablespoons plain flour

2 teaspoons fresh thyme leaves

½ cup (125ml) milk

1 cup (250ml) cream

2 teaspoons wholegrain mustard

2 sheets ready-rolled shortcrust pastry

1 sheet ready-rolled puff pastry

1 egg yolk

1 Bring stock to the boil in medium saucepan. Add chicken; return to the boil. Reduce heat; simmer, covered, about 10 minutes or until chicken is cooked. Remove from heat; stand chicken in poaching liquid 10 minutes. Remove chicken; chop coarsely. Reserve ⅓ cup of the poaching liquid; keep remainder for another use, or discard.

2 Heat oil and butter in medium saucepan; cook leek and celery, stirring, until leek softens. Add flour and thyme; cook, stirring, 1 minute. Gradually stir in reserved poaching liquid, milk and cream; cook, stirring, until mixture boils and thickens. Stir in chicken and mustard. Cool 10 minutes.

3 Preheat oven to 200°C/180°C fan-forced. Oil 1.5-litre (6-cup) ovenproof dish.

4 Line base and side of dish with shortcrust pastry, trim to fit; prick well all over with fork. Bake 10 minutes. Cool 5 minutes. Spoon chicken mixture into pastry case; place puff pastry over filling, trim to fit dish. Brush pastry with egg yolk; cut two small slits in top of pastry. Bake about 20 minutes or until browned lightly.

nutritional count per serving 56g total fat (30.1g saturated fat); 3344kJ (800 cal); 42.5g carbohydrate; 31.1g protein; 3.6g fibre

tournedos with tarragon butter

prep + cook time 30 minutes (+ freezing) **serves** 4

3 medium potatoes (600g)

4 rindless bacon rashers (260g)

4 x 125g beef fillet steaks

tarragon butter

60g butter, softened

1 clove garlic, crushed

2 teaspoons finely chopped fresh tarragon

2 teaspoons finely grated lemon rind

1 Make tarragon butter.

2 Boil, steam or microwave whole potatoes until tender; drain. Cool slightly; slice potatoes thickly.

3 Meanwhile, wrap bacon around beef; secure with toothpicks. Cook beef in heated oiled large frying pan. Cover beef; stand 5 minutes.

4 Meanwhile, add potatoes to same pan; cook until brown.

5 Place potato on serving plates; top with beef then butter slices.

tarragon butter Combine ingredients in small bowl. Place on piece of plastic wrap; shape into 6cm log, wrap tightly. Freeze until firm.

nutritional count per serving 25g total fat (13.2g saturated fat); 2061kJ (493 cal); 17.2g carbohydrate; 48.7g protein; 2.2g fibre

steak diane

prep + cook time 20 minutes serves 4

1 tablespoon olive oil

4 x 125g beef fillet steaks

⅓ cup (80ml) brandy

2 cloves garlic, crushed

¼ cup (60ml) worcestershire sauce

1 cup (250ml) cream

1 tablespoon finely chopped fresh flat-leaf parsley

1 Heat oil in large frying pan; cook steaks. Remove from pan; cover to keep warm.

2 Add brandy to pan; bring to the boil. Add garlic, sauce and cream; cook, stirring, about 3 minutes or until sauce thickens slightly.

3 Remove from heat; stir in parsley. Serve steaks with sauce, and accompany with shoestring chips and a leafy green salad, if you like.

nutritional count per serving 39.1g total fat (21.6g saturated fat); 2182kJ (522 cal); 5.2g carbohydrate; 27.9g protein; 0.4g fibre

greek roast lamb with skordalia and potatoes

prep + cook time 4 hours 50 minutes (+ refrigeration) **serves** 4

2kg leg of lamb
2 cloves garlic, crushed
½ cup (125ml) lemon juice
2 tablespoons olive oil
1 tablespoon fresh oregano leaves
1 teaspoon fresh lemon thyme leaves
5 large potatoes (1.5kg), cut into 3cm cubes
1 tablespoon finely grated lemon rind
2 tablespoons lemon juice, extra
2 tablespoons olive oil, extra
1 teaspoon fresh lemon thyme leaves, extra
skordalia
1 medium potato (200g), quartered
3 cloves garlic, crushed
1 tablespoon lemon juice
1 tablespoon white wine vinegar
2 tablespoons water
⅓ cup (80ml) olive oil

1 Combine lamb with garlic, juice, oil, oregano and thyme in large bowl. Cover; refrigerate 3 hours or overnight.

2 Preheat oven to 160°C/140°C fan-forced.

3 Place lamb in large baking dish; roast, uncovered, 4 hours.

4 Meanwhile, make skordalia.

5 Combine potatoes in large bowl with rind and extra juice, oil and thyme. Place potatoes, in single layer, on oven tray. Roast potatoes for last 30 minutes of lamb cooking time.

6 Remove lamb from oven; cover to keep warm.

7 Increase oven temperature to 220°C/200°C fan-forced; roast potatoes a further 20 minutes or until browned lightly and cooked through. Serve potatoes and lamb with skordalia.

skordalia Boil, steam or microwave potato until tender; drain. Push potato through food mill or fine sieve into medium bowl; cool 10 minutes. Whisk combined garlic, juice, vinegar and the water into potato. Gradually whisk in oil in a thin, steady stream; continue whisking until skordalia thickens. Stir in about a tablespoon of warm water if skordalia is too thick. Serve sprinkled with extra lemon thyme leaves, if you like.

nutritional count per serving 57g total fat (14g saturated fat); 4556kJ (1090 cal); 51.5g carbohydrate; 91.2g protein; 6.7g fibre

roast lamb dinner

prep + cook time 1 hour 40 minutes **serves** 6

2kg leg of lamb

3 sprigs fresh rosemary, chopped coarsely

½ teaspoon sweet paprika

1kg potatoes, chopped coarsely

500g piece pumpkin, chopped coarsely

3 small brown onions (240g), halved

2 tablespoons olive oil

2 tablespoons plain flour

1 cup (250ml) chicken stock

¼ cup (60ml) dry red wine

cauliflower mornay

1 small cauliflower (1kg), cut into florets

50g butter

¼ cup (35g) plain flour

2 cups (500ml) milk

¾ cup (90g) coarsely grated cheddar cheese

1 Preheat oven to 200°C/180°C fan-forced.

2 Place lamb in oiled large baking dish; using sharp knife, score skin at 2cm intervals, sprinkle with rosemary and paprika. Roast lamb 15 minutes.

3 Reduce oven temperature to 180°C/160°C fan-forced; roast lamb about 45 minutes or until cooked as desired.

4 Meanwhile, place potatoes, pumpkin and onions, in single layer, in large shallow baking dish; drizzle with oil. Roast for last 45 minutes of lamb cooking time.

5 Meanwhile, make cauliflower mornay.

6 Remove lamb and vegetables from oven; strain pan juices from lamb into medium jug. Cover lamb and vegetables to keep warm. Return ¼ cup of the pan juices to baking dish, stir in flour; stir over heat about 5 minutes or until mixture bubbles and browns. Gradually add stock and wine; stir over high heat until gravy boils and thickens. Strain gravy into medium heatproof jug.

7 Slice lamb; serve with roasted vegetables, cauliflower mornay and gravy.

cauliflower mornay Boil, steam or microwave cauliflower until tender; drain. Melt butter in medium saucepan, add flour; cook, stirring, until mixture bubbles and thickens. Gradually add milk; cook, stirring, until mixture boils and thickens. Stir in half the cheese. Preheat grill. Place cauliflower in 1.5-litre (6-cup) shallow flameproof dish; pour mornay sauce over cauliflower, sprinkle with remaining cheese. Grill until browned lightly.

nutritional count per serving 35.6g total fat (17g saturated fat); 3244kJ (776 cal); 40.5g carbohydrate; 71.9g protein; 7g fibre

irish stew

prep + cook time 3 hours serves 4

750g lamb neck chops

2 large brown onions (400g), chopped coarsely

1 large carrot (180g), chopped coarsely

1 large parsnip (350g), chopped coarsely

1kg potatoes, chopped coarsely

3½ cups (625ml) beef stock

2 tablespoons tomato paste

1 tablespoon worcestershire sauce

2 sprigs thyme

¼ cup coarsely chopped fresh flat-leaf parsley

1 Preheat oven to 160°C/140°C fan-forced.

2 Layer chops and vegetables in large ovenproof dish; pour over combined stock, paste and sauce. Add thyme.

3 Cook, covered, 2 hours. Uncover; cook 30 minutes or until lamb and vegetables are tender. Serve stew sprinkled with parsley.

nutritional count per serving 19.3g total fat (8.6g saturated fat); 2249kJ (538 cal); 46.8g carbohydrate; 39.7g protein; 8.5g fibre

beef stroganoff

prep + cook time 35 minutes **serves** 4

2 tablespoons vegetable oil

600g beef rump steak, sliced thinly

1 medium brown onion (150g), sliced thinly

2 cloves garlic, crushed

1 teaspoon sweet paprika

400g button mushrooms, sliced thickly

2 tablespoons dry red wine

1 tablespoon lemon juice

2 tablespoons tomato paste

1¼ cups (300g) sour cream

1 tablespoon coarsely chopped fresh dill

1 Heat half the oil in large frying pan; cook beef, in batches, until browned lightly.

2 Heat remaining oil in same pan; cook onion and garlic, stirring, until onion softens. Add paprika and mushrooms; cook, stirring, until mushrooms are tender.

3 Return beef to pan with wine and juice; bring to the boil. Reduce heat; simmer, covered, about 5 minutes or until beef is tender. Add paste, sour cream and dill; cook, stirring, until heated through. Serve stroganoff with steamed rice, mashed potato or fettuccine pasta, if you like.

nutritional count per serving 43.3g total fat (22.4g saturated fat); 2462kJ (589 cal); 5.9g carbohydrate; 41.4g protein; 3.7g fibre

chilli con carne

prep + cook time 3 hours 45 minutes (+ standing) **serves** 8

1 cup (200g) dried kidney beans

1.5kg beef chuck steak

2 litres (8 cups) water

1 tablespoon olive oil

2 medium brown onions (300g), chopped coarsely

2 cloves garlic, crushed

2 teaspoons ground cumin

2 teaspoons ground coriander

½ teaspoon cayenne pepper

2 teaspoons sweet paprika

2 x 400g cans crushed tomatoes

1 tablespoon tomato paste

4 green onions, chopped coarsely

2 tablespoons coarsely chopped fresh coriander

⅓ cup (65g) finely chopped bottled jalapeño chillies

1 Place beans in medium bowl, cover with water; stand overnight, drain.

2 Combine beef with the water in large saucepan; bring to the boil. Reduce heat, simmer, covered, 1½ hours.

3 Drain beef in large muslin-lined strainer over bowl; reserve 3½ cups (875ml) of the cooking liquid. Using two forks, shred beef.

4 Heat oil in same pan; cook brown onion and garlic, stirring, until onion is soft. Add spices; cook, stirring, until fragrant. Add beans, undrained tomatoes, paste and 2 cups of the reserved liquid; bring to the boil. Reduce heat, simmer, covered, 1 hour.

5 Add beef and remaining reserved liquid to pan; simmer, covered, about 30 minutes or until beans are tender. Remove from heat; stir in green onions, coriander and chilli. Serve chilli con carne with steamed rice, if you like.

nutritional count per serving 11.4g total fat (3.9g saturated fat); 1496kJ (358 cal); 14.7g carbohydrate; 45.1g protein; 7.6g fibre

roast loin of pork with apple sauce

prep + cook time 2 hours **serves** 8

Ask your butcher to roll and tie the pork at 2cm intervals for you, and to score the rind, if it isn't already done so.

2 sprigs rosemary
2.5kg boneless loin of pork, rind on
1 tablespoon olive oil
1 tablespoon coarse cooking salt
apple sauce
3 large apples (600g)
¼ cup (60ml) water
1 teaspoon white sugar
pinch ground cinnamon

1 Preheat oven to 250°C/230°C fan-forced.
2 Tuck the rosemary into the string under the pork. Place pork in large baking dish; rub rind with oil then salt. Roast about 40 minutes or until rind blisters. Drain excess fat from dish.
3 Reduce oven temperature to 180°C/160°C fan-forced. Roast pork about 1 hour.
4 Meanwhile, make apple sauce.
5 Transfer pork to plate; cover loosely, stand 15 minutes before carving. Serve pork with apple sauce.
apple sauce Peel and core apples; slice thickly. Place apple and the water in medium saucepan; simmer, covered, 5 minutes, uncover; simmer, about 5 minutes or until apple is soft. Remove from heat, stir in sugar and cinnamon.

nutritional count per serving 72g total fat (24.1g saturated fat); 3762kJ (900 cal); 7.7g carbohydrate; 56.7g protein; 1.1g fibre

pork chops with apples and calvados

prep + cook time 30 minutes **serves** 4

Calvados is an expensive apple brandy – use brandy instead of calvados if you like.

4 x 280g pork loin chops
50g butter
2 medium apples (300g), peeled, cut into thin wedges
4 shallots (100g), sliced thinly
1 tablespoon plain flour
½ cup (125ml) calvados
1 cup (250ml) cider vinegar
1 cup (250ml) chicken stock
⅔ cup (160ml) cream

1 Cook pork in heated oiled large frying pan. Remove from pan; cover to keep warm. Drain and discard excess fat from pan.

2 Heat half the butter in pan; cook apples, stirring, until browned lightly. Remove from pan.

3 Heat remaining butter in pan; cook shallots, stirring, until soft. Add flour; cook, stirring, 1 minute. Add calvados; bring to the boil. Stir in cider, stock and cream; simmer, uncovered, until sauce thickens slightly. Return apples to pan; cook until heated through.

4 Serve pork topped with apples and sauce; accompany with a green salad, if you like.

nutritional count per serving 47.5g total fat (25g saturated fat); 2947kJ (705 cal); 18.1g carbohydrate; 35.7g protein; 1.4g fibre

Classic
Desserts

crème caramel

prep + cook time 1 hour (+ refrigeration) **serves** 8

¾ cup (165g) caster sugar

½ cup (125ml) water

6 eggs

1 teaspoon vanilla extract

⅓ cup (75g) caster sugar, extra

300ml cream

1¾ cups (430ml) milk

1 Preheat oven to 160°C/140°C fan-forced.

2 Combine sugar and the water in medium heavy-based frying pan; stir over heat, without boiling, until sugar dissolves. Bring to the boil; boil, uncovered, without stirring, until mixture is a deep caramel colour. Remove from heat; allow bubbles to subside. Pour toffee into deep 20cm-round cake pan.

3 Whisk eggs, extract and extra sugar in large bowl.

4 Combine cream and milk in medium saucepan; bring to the boil. Whisking constantly, pour hot milk mixture into egg mixture. Strain mixture into cake pan.

5 Place pan in baking dish; add enough boiling water to come half way up side of pan. Bake, in oven, about 40 minutes or until set. Remove custard from baking dish, cover; refrigerate overnight.

6 Gently ease crème caramel from side of pan; invert onto deep-sided serving plate.

nutritional count per serving 22.3g total fat (13.3g saturated fat); 1526kJ (365 cal); 33.8g carbohydrate; 7.5g protein; 0g fibre

apple pie

prep + cook time 1 hour 45 minutes (+ refrigeration) **serves** 8

10 medium apples (1.5kg)

½ cup (125ml) water

¼ cup (55g) caster sugar

1 teaspoon finely grated lemon rind

¼ teaspoon ground cinnamon

1 egg white

1 tablespoon caster sugar, extra

pastry

1 cup (150g) plain flour

½ cup (75g) self-raising flour

¼ cup (35g) cornflour

¼ cup (30g) custard powder

1 tablespoon caster sugar

100g cold butter, chopped coarsely

1 egg yolk

¼ cup (60ml) iced water

1 Make pastry.

2 Peel, core and slice apple thickly. Place apple and the water in large saucepan; bring to the boil. Reduce heat; simmer, covered, about 10 minutes or until apples soften. Drain; stir in sugar, rind and cinnamon. Cool.

3 Preheat oven to 220°C/200°C fan-forced. Grease deep 25cm pie dish.

4 Divide pastry in half. Roll one half between sheets of baking paper until large enough to line dish. Lift pastry into dish; press into base and side. Spoon apple mixture into pastry case; brush edge with egg white.

5 Roll remaining pastry large enough to cover filling; lift onto filling. Press edges together; trim away excess pastry. Brush pastry with egg white; sprinkle with extra sugar. Bake 20 minutes. Reduce oven temperature to 180°C/160°C fan-forced; bake about 25 minutes or until golden brown. Serve with vanilla custard, or scoops of vanilla ice-cream, if you like.

pastry Process dry ingredients with the butter until crumbly. Add egg yolk and the water; process until combined. Knead on floured surface until smooth. Cover; refrigerate 30 minutes.

nutritional count per serving 11.4g total fat (7g saturated fat); 1438kJ (344 cal); 53.9g carbohydrate; 4.3g protein; 3.7g fibre

chocolate mousse

prep + cook time 35 minutes (+ refrigeration) serves 6

200g dark eating chocolate, chopped coarsely
30g unsalted butter
3 eggs, separated (*see note, below*)
300ml thickened cream, whipped

1 Melt chocolate and butter in large glass heatproof bowl over large saucepan of simmering water (do not allow water to touch base of bowl). Remove from heat. Stir in egg yolks; cool.
2 Beat egg whites in small bowl with electric mixer until soft peaks form.
3 Meanwhile, fold cream into chocolate mixture then fold in egg whites in two batches.
4 Divide mousse among serving dishes; refrigerate 3 hours or overnight. Serve topped with whipped cream and chocolate curls, if you like.

nutritional count per serving 34.8g total fat (21.4g saturated fat); 1777kJ (425 cal); 22.5g carbohydrate; 6.1g protein; 0.4g fibre

The eggs must be at room temperature for success with this recipe.

lemon delicious pudding

prep + cook time 1 hour **serves** 6

125g butter, melted

2 teaspoons finely grated lemon rind

1½ cups (330g) caster sugar

3 eggs, separated

½ cup (75g) self-raising flour

⅓ cup (80ml) lemon juice

1⅓ cups (330ml) milk

1 Preheat oven to 180°C/160°C fan-forced. Grease six 1-cup (250ml) ovenproof dishes; place in large baking dish.

2 Combine butter, rind, sugar and yolks in large bowl. Whisk in sifted flour then juice. Gradually whisk in milk; mixture should be smooth and runny.

3 Beat egg whites in small bowl with electric mixer until soft peaks form; fold into lemon mixture in two batches.

4 Divide lemon mixture among dishes. Add enough boiling water to baking dish to come halfway up side of ovenproof dishes. Bake about 30 minutes or until puddings have risen and are a light golden colour.

nutritional count per serving 22g total fat (13.5g saturated fat); 2069kJ (495 cal); 67.1g carbohydrate; 6.7g protein; 0.5g fibre

bread and butter pudding

prep + cook time 1 hour 15 minutes **serves** 6

6 slices white bread (270g)
40g butter, softened
½ cup (80g) sultanas
¼ teaspoon ground nutmeg
custard
1½ cups (375ml) milk
2 cups (500ml) cream
⅓ cup (75g) caster sugar
1 teaspoon vanilla extract
4 eggs

1 Preheat oven to 160°C/140°C fan-forced. Grease shallow 2-litre (8-cup) ovenproof dish.

2 Make custard.

3 Trim crusts from bread. Spread each slice with butter; cut into four triangles. Layer bread, overlapping, in dish; sprinkle with sultanas. Pour custard over bread; sprinkle with nutmeg.

4 Place ovenproof dish in large baking dish; add enough boiling water to come halfway up side of ovenproof dish. Bake about 45 minutes or until pudding is set. Remove pudding from baking dish; stand 5 minutes before serving. Serve dusted with sifted icing sugar, if you like.

custard Combine milk, cream, sugar and extract in medium saucepan; bring to the boil. Whisk eggs in large bowl; whisking constantly, gradually add hot milk mixture to egg mixture.

nutritional count per serving 48.6g total fat (30.4g saturated fat); 2859kJ (684 cal); 49.3g carbohydrate; 12.4g protein; 1.8g fibre

marshmallow pavlova

prep + cook time 1 hour 50 minutes (+ cooling) **serves** 8

4 egg whites
1 cup (220g) caster sugar
½ teaspoon vanilla extract
¾ teaspoon white vinegar
300ml thickened cream, whipped
250g strawberries, halved
¼ cup (60ml) passionfruit pulp

1 Preheat oven to 120°C/100°C fan-forced. Line oven tray with foil; grease foil, dust with cornflour, shake away excess. Mark 18cm-circle on foil.

2 Beat egg whites in small bowl with electric mixer until soft peaks form; gradually add sugar, beating until sugar dissolves. Add extract and vinegar; beat until combined.

3 Spread meringue into circle on foil, building up at the side to 8cm in height. Smooth side and top of pavlova gently. Using spatula blade, mark decorative grooves around side of pavlova; smooth top again.

4 Bake pavlova about 1½ hours. Turn oven off; cool pavlova in oven with door ajar.

5 Cut around top edge of pavlova (the crisp meringue top will fall on top of the marshmallow centre). Serve pavlova topped with whipped cream, strawberries and passionfruit.

nutritional count per serving 14g total fat (9.2g saturated fat); 1095kJ (262 cal); 30g carbohydrate; 3.3g protein; 1.7g fibre

summer pudding

prep + cook time 35 minutes (+ refrigeration) **serves** 6

⅓ cup (75g) caster sugar
½ cup (125ml) water
2 cups (300g) frozen blackberries
3⅓ cups (500g) frozen mixed berries
6 thick slices stale white bread (460g)
¼ cup (80g) blackberry jam

1 Combine sugar and the water in medium saucepan; bring to the boil. Stir in berries; return to the boil. Reduce heat; simmer, uncovered, until berries soften. Strain over medium bowl; reserve syrup and berries separately.
2 Line 1.25-litre (5-cup) pudding bowl with plastic wrap, extending wrap 10cm over side of bowl. Remove crusts from bread. Cut two semi-circles from two slices of bread slightly smaller than the top edge of the bowl. Cut one round from one bread slice to fit the base of the bowl. Cut remaining bread into 10cm long strips.

3 Place small bread round in base of bowl; use bread strips to line side of bowl.
4 Pour ⅔ cup of the reserved syrup into small jug; reserve. Fill pudding bowl with berries; cover with remaining syrup, top with large bread rounds. Cover pudding with overhanging plastic wrap, weight pudding with saucer; refrigerate 3 hours or overnight.
5 Stir jam and two tablespoons of the reserved syrup in small saucepan until heated through. Turn pudding onto serving plate; brush with remaining reserved syrup then jam mixture. Serve with extra fresh berries and whipped cream, if you like.

nutritional count per serving 2.2g total fat (0.3g saturated fat); 1346kJ (322 cal); 62.2g carbohydrate; 8.6g protein; 7.4g fibre

crêpes suzette

prep + cook time 1 hour 40 minutes (+ standing) **serves** 4

¾ cup (110g) plain flour

3 eggs

2 tablespoons vegetable oil

¾ cup (180ml) milk

orange sauce

125g unsalted butter

½ cup (110g) caster sugar

1½ cups (375ml) orange juice

2 tablespoons lemon juice

⅓ cup (80ml) orange-flavoured liqueur

1 Sift flour into medium bowl, make well in centre; add eggs and oil then gradually whisk in milk until smooth. Pour batter into large jug, cover; stand 1 hour.

2 Heat greased heavy-based crêpe pan or small frying pan; pour ¼ cup of batter into pan, tilting pan to coat base. Cook, over low heat, until browned lightly, loosening edge of crêpe with spatula. Turn crêpe; brown other side. Remove crêpe from pan; cover to keep warm. Repeat with remaining batter to make a total of 8 crêpes, greasing pan each time.

3 Make orange sauce. Fold crêpes in half then in half again, place in sauce; warm over low heat.

4 Remove crêpes to serving plates; pour hot sauce over crêpes. Serve with orange segments, if you like.

orange sauce Melt butter in large frying pan, add sugar; cook, stirring, until mixture begins to brown. Add strained juices; bring to the boil. Reduce heat; simmer, uncovered, about 3 minutes or until a golden colour. Remove from heat; add liqueur, ignite.

nutritional count per serving 41g total fat (20.5g saturated fat); 3039kJ (727 cal); 66.9g carbohydrate; 10.3g protein; 1.3g fibre

Make sure overhead exhaust fans are turned off before igniting the orange sauce.

Be very careful when igniting the sauce – use extra long matches, available from supermarkets or camping stores. Igniting the sauce burns off the alcohol, leaving a more intense flavour. If you prefer, the sauce can be served as is, without first igniting it.

new york cheesecake

prep + cook time 2 hours 30 minutes (+ refrigeration & cooling) serves 12

250g plain sweet biscuits

125g butter, melted

750g cream cheese, softened

2 teaspoons finely grated orange rind

1 teaspoon finely grated lemon rind

1 cup (220g) caster sugar

3 eggs

¾ cup (180g) sour cream

¼ cup (60ml) lemon juice

sour cream topping

1 cup (240g) sour cream

2 tablespoons caster sugar

2 teaspoons lemon juice

1 Process biscuits until fine. Add butter, process until combined. Press mixture over base and side of 24cm springform tin. Place tin on oven tray; refrigerate 30 minutes.

2 Preheat oven to 180°C/160°C fan-forced.

3 Beat cream cheese, rinds and sugar in medium bowl with electric mixer until smooth. Beat in eggs, one at a time, then sour cream and juice.

4 Pour filling into tin; bake 1¼ hours. Remove from oven; cool 15 minutes.

5 Make sour cream topping; spread over cheesecake. Bake cheesecake 20 minutes; cool in oven with door ajar. Refrigerate cheesecake 3 hours or overnight.

sour cream topping Combine ingredients in small bowl.

nutritional count per serving 47.8g total fat (30.1g saturated fat); 2587kJ (619 cal); 39g carbohydrate; 9.2g protein; 0.4g fibre

tiramisu

prep time 30 minutes (+ refrigeration) **serves** 8

2 tablespoons ground espresso coffee

1 cup (250ml) boiling water

½ cup (125ml) marsala

250g packet sponge finger biscuits

300ml thickened cream

¼ cup (40g) icing sugar

2 cups (500g) mascarpone cheese

2 tablespoons marsala, extra

2 teaspoons cocoa powder

1 Combine coffee and the water in coffee plunger; stand 2 minutes before plunging. Combine coffee mixture and marsala in medium heatproof bowl; cool 10 minutes.

2 Place half the biscuits, in single layer, over base of deep 2-litre (8-cup) dish; drizzle with half the coffee mixture.

3 Beat cream and sifted icing sugar in small bowl until soft peaks form; transfer to large bowl. Fold in combined mascarpone cheese and extra marsala.

4 Spread half the cream mixture over biscuits in dish. Submerge the remaining biscuits, one at a time, in coffee mixture, taking care the biscuits do not become so soggy that they fall apart; place over cream layer. Top biscuit layer with the remaining cream mixture. Cover; refrigerate 3 hours or overnight.

5 Serve tiramisu dusted with sifted cocoa.

nutritional count per serving 45g total fat (29.9g saturated fat); 2391kJ (572 cal); 25.8g carbohydrate; 6.5g protein; 0.5g fibre

109

chocolate tart

prep + cook time 1 hour 30 minutes (+ refrigeration) serves 8

1½ cups (225g) plain flour

½ cup (110g) caster sugar

140g cold butter, chopped coarsely

1 egg, beaten lightly

1 teaspoon cocoa powder

chocolate filling

2 eggs

2 egg yolks

¼ cup (55g) caster sugar

250g dark eating chocolate, melted

200g butter, melted

1 Process flour, sugar and butter until crumbly; add egg, process until ingredients come together. Knead dough on floured surface until smooth. Cover; refrigerate 30 minutes.

2 Roll pastry between sheets of baking paper until large enough to line greased 24cm-round loose-based flan tin. Lift pastry into tin; press into base and side, trim edge, prick base all over with fork. Cover; refrigerate 30 minutes.

3 Meanwhile, preheat oven to 200°C/180°C fan-forced.

4 Make chocolate filling.

5 Place flan tin on oven tray; cover pastry with baking paper, fill with dried beans or rice. Bake 10 minutes. Remove paper and beans carefully from tin; bake about 5 minutes or until pastry has browned lightly. Cool.

6 Reduce oven temperature to 180°C/160°C fan-forced.

7 Pour chocolate filling into pastry case. Bake about 10 minutes or until filling has set; cool 10 minutes. Refrigerate 1 hour. Serve dusted with sifted cocoa powder. Serve tart topped with berries of your choice, if you like. We used strawberries.

chocolate filling Whisk eggs, egg yolks and sugar in medium heatproof bowl over medium saucepan of simmering water (don't let water touch base of bowl) about 15 minutes or until light and fluffy. Gently whisk chocolate and butter into egg mixture.

nutritional count per serving 48.1g total fat (32.7g saturated fat); 2934kJ (702 cal); 59.1g carbohydrate; 7.9g protein; 2.5g fibre

Classic Stocks

These recipes can be made up to 4 days ahead; refrigerate overnight then remove any fat from the surface. Keep stock, covered, in the refrigerator. All the recipes make approximately 2.5 litres (10 cups).

beef stock

prep + cook time 5 hours 30 minutes (+ refrigeration)

2kg meaty beef bones
2 medium onions (300g), unpeeled, chopped coarsely
2 stalks celery (300g), chopped coarsely
2 medium carrots (240g), chopped coarsely
3 bay leaves
2 teaspoons black peppercorns
5 litres (20 cups) water
3 litres (12 cups) water, extra

1 Preheat oven to 220°C/200°C fan-forced.
2 Place bones and onion in baking dish. Bake about 1 hour or until well browned.
3 Transfer bones and onion to large saucepan, add the celery, carrot, bay leaves, peppercorns and the water; bring to the boil. Reduce heat; simmer, uncovered, 3 hours. Add the extra water; simmer, uncovered, about 1 hour. Strain into large heatproof bowl; cool then refrigerate.

nutritional count per cup (250ml) 0.6g total fat
(0.2g saturated fat); 134kJ (32 cal);
2.8g carbohydrate; 2.9g protein; 1.7g fibre

chicken stock

prep + cook time 2 hours 10 minutes (+ refrigeration)

2kg chicken bones
2 medium onions (300g), chopped coarsely
2 stalks celery (300g), chopped coarsely
2 medium carrots (240g), chopped coarsely
3 bay leaves
2 teaspoons black peppercorns
5 litres (20 cups) water

1 Combine ingredients in large saucepan; bring to the boil. Reduce heat; simmer, uncovered, about 2 hours.
2 Strain into large heatproof bowl; cool then refrigerate.

nutritional count per cup (250ml) 0.9g total fat
(0.3g saturated fat); 146kJ (35 cal);
3.2g carbohydrate; 2.7g protein; 1.5g fibre

fish stock

prep + cook time 30 minutes (+ refrigeration)

1.5kg fish bones
3 litres (12 cups) water
1 medium onion (150g), chopped coarsely
2 stalks celery (300g), chopped coarsely
2 bay leaves
1 teaspoon black peppercorns

1 Combine ingredients in large saucepan; bring to the boil. Reduce heat; simmer, uncovered, about 20 minutes.
2 Strain into large heatproof bowl; cool then refrigerate.

nutritional count per cup (250ml) 0.2g total fat (0.1g saturated fat); 63kJ (15 cal); 1g carbohydrate; 1.9g protein; 0.8g fibre

vegetable stock

prep + cook time 1 hour 40 minutes (+ refrigeration)

2 large carrots (360g), chopped coarsely
2 large parsnips (700g), chopped coarsely
4 medium onions (600g), chopped coarsely
10 stalks celery (1.5kg), chopped coarsely
4 bay leaves
2 teaspoons black peppercorns
6 litres (24 cups) water

1 Combine ingredients in large saucepan; bring to the boil. Reduce heat; simmer, uncovered, about 1½ hours.
2 Strain into large heatproof bowl; cool then refrigerate.

nutritional count per cup (250ml) 0.3g total fat (0g saturated fat); 276kJ (66 cal); 11.6g carbohydrate; 2.4g protein; 3.8g fibre

Glossary

ALMOND flat, pointy-ended nut with a pitted brown shell enclosing a creamy white kernel covered by a brown skin.
blanched brown skins removed.
essence also known as extract.
flaked paper-thin slices.
slivered small lengthways-cut pieces.

BACON RASHERS also known as slices of bacon.

BARLEY a nutritious grain used in soups and stews. Hulled barley, the least processed form of barley, is high in fibre.
pearl barley has had the husk removed then been hulled and polished so that only the "pearl" of the original grain remains, much the same as white rice.

BASIL an aromatic herb; there are many types, but the most commonly used is sweet, or common, basil.

BEANS
kidney medium-sized red bean, slightly floury in texture yet sweet in flavour; sold dried or canned.
white in this book, some recipes may simply call for "white beans", a generic term we use for canned or dried navy, cannellini, haricot or great northern beans – all of which can be substituted for each other.

BEEF
chuck steak taken from the shoulder; isn't as tender as other cuts of beef, therefore it needs slow-roasting to achieve the best results.
topside roast a large hindquarter cut used for roasting.
gravy also known as shin beef. A cut from the lower leg; commonly used in stews and braises.

BEETROOT also known as red beets or beets; firm, round root vegetable.

BICARBONATE OF SODA also known as carb or baking soda; used as a leavening agent in baking.

BISCUITS, PLAIN SWEET also known as cookies; a crisp sweet biscuit without icing or any fillings.

BRAN, UNPROCESSED made from the outer layer of a cereal, most often the husks of wheat, rice or oats.

BREADCRUMBS, STALE one- or two-day-old bread made into crumbs by blending or processing.

BUTTER use salted or unsalted (sweet) butter as directed by the recipe; 125g is equal to one stick (4 ounces) of butter.
clarified butter, see ghee.

BUTTERMILK originally the term given to the slightly sour liquid left after butter was churned from cream, today it is commercially made similarly to yogurt. Sold alongside all fresh milk products in supermarkets. Despite the implication of its name, it is low in fat.

CALVADOS an expensive apple brandy; use brandy instead of Calvados if you like.

CAPERS the grey-green buds of a warm climate (usually Mediterranean) shrub, sold either dried and salted or pickled in a vinegar brine. Baby capers, those picked early, are smaller, fuller-flavoured and more expensive than the full-sized ones. Rinse well before using.

CAPSICUM also known as bell pepper or, simply, pepper. Membranes and seeds should be discarded before use.

CAYENNE PEPPER a thin-fleshed, long and extremely hot red chilli usually sold dried and ground.

CHEESE
cheddar a semi-hard cows-milk cheese. It ranges in colour from white to pale yellow, and has a slightly crumbly texture if properly matured.
cream commonly known as Philadelphia or Philly, a soft cows-milk cheese. Also available as spreadable light cream cheese, which is a blend of cottage and cream cheeses.
gruyère a hard-rind swiss cheese with small holes and a nutty, slightly salty flavour. A popular cheese for soufflés.
mascarpone a buttery-rich, cream-like cheese made from cows milk. Ivory-coloured, soft and delicate, with the texture of softened butter, mascarpone is one of the traditional ingredients in tiramisu and other Italian desserts.
mozzarella a soft, spun-curd cheese. It has a low melting point and a wonderfully elastic texture when heated; used to add texture rather than flavour.
parmesan also known as parmigiano; a hard, grainy cows-milk cheese. The curd is salted in brine for a month before being aged for up to two years in humid conditions.
pecorino the generic Italian name for cheeses made from sheep milk; hard, white to pale-yellow cheeses.
romano this Italian hard cheese was originally made from sheep milk, however it is now available made from cows milk. Straw-coloured and grainy in texture, it's mainly used for grating. Parmesan can be substituted.

swiss a generic name for a variety of cheeses originating in Switzerland, among them emmentaler and gruyère.

CHERVIL also known as cicily; a herb with a mild fennel flavour and curly dark-green leaves.

CHILLI available in many types and sizes. Use rubber gloves when seeding and chopping fresh chillies as they can burn your skin. Removing seeds and membranes lessens the heat level.
long red available both fresh and dried; a generic term used for any moderately hot, long (about 6-8cm), thin chilli.
jalapeño fairly hot green chillies, available from specialty greengrocers. Sold finely chopped or whole, bottled in vinegar, as well as fresh; we use the medium-hot, sweetish chopped bottled version unless directed otherwise.
red thai small, very hot, and bright red in colour.

CHIPOLATA also known as "little fingers"; highly spiced, coarse-textured beef sausage.

CHIVES related to the onion and leek, with a subtle onion flavour. Chives and flowering chives are interchangeable.

CHOCOLATE, DARK EATING made of cocoa liquor, cocoa butter and sugar.

CHORIZO a sausage of Spanish origin, made of coarsely ground pork and highly seasoned with garlic and chillies.

CINNAMON dried inner bark of the shoots of the cinnamon tree; available in stick (quill) or ground form.

COCOA POWDER also known as cocoa; unsweetened, dried, roasted then ground cocoa beans.

CORIANDER also known as pak chee, cilantro or chinese parsley; bright-green leafy herb with a pungent flavour. Both the stems and roots of coriander are used in Thai cooking; wash well before using. Coriander seeds are also available but are no substitute for fresh coriander, as the tastes are very different.

CORNFLOUR also known as cornstarch; used as a thickening agent in cooking.

CREAM we use fresh cream, also known as pure cream and pouring cream, unless otherwise stated; it has no additives.
sour a thick commercially-cultured soured cream. Minimum fat content 35%.
thickened a whipping cream containing a thickener. Minimum fat content 35%.

CUCUMBERS

lebanese short, slender and thin-skinned. Probably the most popular variety because of its tender, edible skin, tiny, yielding seeds and sweet, fresh and flavoursome taste.

telegraph long and green with ridges running down its entire length; also known as continental cucumber.

CUMIN also known as zeera or comino; the dried seed of a plant related to the parsley family having a spicy, nutty flavour. Available in seed form or dried and ground.

CURRANTS, DRIED tiny, almost black raisins so-named after a grape variety that originated in Corinth, Greece.

CURRY POWDER a blend of ground spices used when making Indian food. May include dried chilli, cinnamon, coriander, cumin, fennel, fenugreek, mace, cardamom and turmeric. Choose mild or hot blends to suit your taste and the recipe.

CUSTARD POWDER instant mixture used to make pouring custard; similar to North American instant pudding mixes.

DATES are green when unripe and turn yellow, golden brown, mahogany red or black – depending on the variety – as they ripen. Available fresh or dried, pitted or unpitted. The skin is thin and papery and the flesh is extremely sweet. Choose plump, soft dates with a smooth, shiny skin. As the date fruit dries, the sugars will concentrate in the dense, moist flesh, ultimately forming sugar crystals on the outside of the date – when this occurs, the date is usually less than ideal to eat, as the flesh will be dry and leathery.

DILL also known as dill weed; used fresh or dried, in seed form or ground. It has a sweet anise/celery flavour. Its distinctive feathery, frond-like fresh leaves are grassier and more subtle than the dried version or the seeds.

DILL PICKLE a small cucumber preserved in brine or vinegar flavoured with dill seed.

EGGPLANT purple-skinned vegetable also known as aubergine.

EGGS if recipes in this book call for raw or barely cooked eggs, exercise caution if there is a salmonella problem in your area.

ENGLISH MUFFINS are a more bread-like version of the crumpet. Should be split in half before using.

FENNEL BULB also known as anise or finocchio; a white to pale green-white, crisp, roundish vegetable about 8-12cm in diameter. The bulb has a slightly sweet, anise flavour but the leaves have a much stronger taste. Also the name given to dried seeds having a licorice flavour.

FLOUR

plain an all-purpose flour made from wheat.

self-raising plain flour sifted with baking powder in the proportion of 1 cup flour to 2 teaspoons baking powder.

FRENCH STICK bread that's been formed into a long, narrow cylindrical loaf. It usually has a crisp brown crust and a light chewy interior. A standard stick is 5-6cm wide and 3-4cm tall, but it can be up to a metre in length. It is also known as french bread, french loaf or baguette.

GHEE also known as clarified butter, ghee is butter that has been purified by removing the milk solids. It retains the lovely taste of butter, but can be heated to a higher temperature without burning. You can clarify butter yourself by melting unsalted butter in a small saucepan over medium heat. Skim and discard any foam from the top, then ladle off the clear butter, leaving the white milk solids in the base of the pan (or strain the liquid through a cheesecloth-lined strainer). The clarified butter can be stored in the fridge like regular butter. Alternatively, ghee is now sold alongside butter in most major supermarkets.

GLOBE ARTICHOKES large flower-bud of a member of the thistle family. Has tough petal-like leaves; edible in part when cooked.

HERBS we specify when to use fresh or dried herbs in this book. Dried (not ground) herbs can be used in the proportion of one to four, i.e., use 1 teaspoon dried herbs instead of 4 teaspoons (1 tablespoon) chopped fresh herbs.

JAM also known as preserve or conserve.

JUNIPER BERRIES the dried fruit from the evergreen tree of the same name; can be found in specialty spice stores and better delicatessens. Provides the distinctive flavour to gin.

KITCHEN STRING made of a natural product, such as cotton or hemp, so that it neither affects the flavour of the food it's tied around nor melts when heated.

LAMB NECK CHOPS one of the tougher cuts and is therefore one of the cheaper ones. The meat is often more fatty than other cuts and is usually used in stews and casseroles.

LEEK a member of the onion family; resembles the green onion but is much larger and more subtle in flavour.

LETTUCE

butter have small, round, loosely formed heads with soft, buttery-textured leaves ranging from pale green on the outer leaves to pale yellow-green on the inner leaves. Has a sweet flavour.

cos also known as romaine lettuce; the traditional caesar salad lettuce. Long, with leaves ranging from dark green on the outside to almost white near the core; the leaves have a stiff centre rib that gives a slight cupping effect to the leaf on either side.

oak leaf also known as feuille de chene. Available in both red and green leaf.

iceberg a heavy, firm, round lettuce with tightly packed leaves and a crisp texture.

MAPLE SYRUP a thin syrup distilled from the sap of the maple tree. Maple-flavoured syrup or pancake syrup is not an adequate substitute for the real thing.

MARSALA a fortified wine, originally produced on the island of Sicily, to which additional alcohol has been added, most commonly in the form of brandy (a spirit distilled from wine). It is available in a range of styles, from sweet to dry.

MINCE also known as ground meat.

MUSHROOMS

button small, cultivated white mushrooms having a delicate, subtle flavour.

swiss brown also known as cremini or roman; light to dark brown mushrooms with full-bodied flavour. Button or cup mushrooms can be substituted.

MUSTARD

dijon pale brown, distinctively flavoured, fairly mild-tasting french mustard.

wholegrain also known as seeded mustard; a coarse-grain mustard made from black/brown and yellow mustard seeds and dijon-style mustard.

NUTMEG the dried nut of an evergreen tree native to Indonesia; it is available in ground form or you can grate your own with a fine grater.

OIL

olive made from ripened olives. Extra virgin and virgin are the best, while extra light or light refers to taste not fat levels.

115

vegetable sourced from plants rather than animal fats.

ONIONS

green also known as scallion or, incorrectly, shallot; an immature onion picked before the bulb has formed, having a long, bright-green edible stalk.

red also known as spanish, red spanish or bermuda onion; a sweet-flavoured, large, purple-red onion.

shallots also called french shallots, golden shallots or eschalots; small, brown-skinned, elongated members of the onion family. Grows in tight clusters similar to garlic.

spring has small white bulbs and narrow, long, green-leafed tops.

ORANGE-FLAVOURED LIQUEUR

we used Grand Marnier, but you can use your favourite brand.

OREGANO also known as wild marjoram; has a pungent, peppery flavour. Available fresh or dried.

PANCETTA an Italian unsmoked bacon rolled into a sausage shape and dried for several weeks.

PAPRIKA ground, dried, sweet red capsicum (bell pepper); there are many types available, including sweet, hot, mild and smoked.

PARSLEY, FLAT-LEAF also known as continental parsley or italian parsley.

PASTA

fettuccine meaning "little ribbons" in Italian, this thin flat pasta is about 1cm wide; goes well with cream sauces.

macaroni tube-shaped pasta available in various sizes.

shell shell-shaped ranging from tiny to very large.

spaghetti long, thin solid strands of pasta.

PASTRY, READY-ROLLED

puff packaged sheets of frozen puff pastry, available from supermarkets.

shortcrust packaged sheets of shortcrust pastry, available from supermarkets.

PROSCIUTTO cured, unsmoked (air-dried), pressed ham.

RICE

calasparra a short-grain rice available from Spanish delicatessens and gourmet-food stores. If you can't find calasparra, any short-grain rice can be substituted.

long-grain elongated grain, remains separate when cooked; most popular steaming rice in Asia.

ROLLED OATS oat groats (oats that have been husked) steamed-softened, flattened with rollers, dried and packaged for consumption as a cereal product.

SAFFRON THREADS available in strands or ground form; imparts a yellow-orange colour to food once infused. Quality varies greatly; the best is the most expensive spice in the world. Should be stored in the freezer.

SAGE pungent herb with narrow, grey-green leaves; slightly bitter with a light musty mint aroma.

SAUCES

Tabasco brand name of an extremely fiery sauce made from vinegar, hot red thai chillies and salt.

tomato also known as ketchup or catsup; a flavoured condiment made from tomatoes, vinegar and spices.

worcestershire a thin, dark-brown spicy sauce made from garlic, soy sauce, lime, tamarind, onions, molasses, anchovies, vinegar and seasonings.

SAVOIARDI also known as Savoy biscuits, lady's fingers or sponge fingers; are long, oval-shaped Italian-style crisp fingers made from sponge-cake mixture.

SEAFOOD

blue swimmer crabs also known as sand crabs or atlantic blue crabs.

firm white fish fillets blue eye, bream, flathead, swordfish, ling, whiting, cod, jewfish, snapper, haddock or sea perch are all good choices. Check for any small pieces of bone in the fillets and use tweezers to remove them.

mussels buy from a fish market where there is reliably fresh fish; they must be tightly closed when bought, indicating they are alive. Before cooking, scrub the shells with a strong brush and remove the "beards". Discard any shells that do not open during cooking.

prawns also known as shrimp.

salmon red-pink firm fleshed fish with a moist delicate flavour and few bones.

scallops a bivalve mollusc with a fluted shell valve; we use scallops that have the coral (roe) attached.

SHALLOTS see onions.

SPLIT PEAS also known as field peas; green or yellow pulse split along a centre seam. Grown especially for drying.

SUGAR

brown a very soft, finely granulated sugar retaining molasses for its characteristic colour and flavour.

caster also known as superfine or finely granulated table sugar.

icing also known as confectioners' sugar or powdered sugar; granulated sugar crushed together with a small amount of cornflour added.

white a coarsely granulated table sugar, also known as crystal sugar.

SULTANAS dried grapes, also known as golden raisins.

TARRAGON an aromatic herb with an anise-like flavour; available fresh, dried and powdered.

THYME a member of the mint family; has tiny grey-green leaves that give off a pungent minty, light-lemon aroma.

lemon thyme a herb with a lemony scent, which is due to the high level of citral (an oil also found in lemon, orange, verbena and lemon grass) in its leaves. The citrus scent is enhanced by crushing the leaves in your hands before using the herb.

TOMATO

chutney a condiment containing tomatoes and other vegetables, sugar, vinegar and spices.

paste triple-concentrated tomato puree used to flavour soups, stews, sauces and casseroles.

puree canned puréed tomatoes (not tomato paste). Substitute with fresh peeled and puréed tomatoes.

VEAL

osso buco literally meaning "bone with a hole", osso buco is cut from the shin of the hind leg. It is also known as knuckle.

schnitzel thinly sliced steak available crumbed or plain (uncrumbed); we use plain schnitzel, sometimes called escalopes, in our recipes.

steaks lean steak cut from a sirloin roast.

VINEGAR

balsamic originally from Modena, Italy, and made from the juice of Trebbiano grapes; it is a deep rich brown colour with a sweet and sour flavour. There are now many balsamic vinegars on the market ranging in pungency and quality depending on how, and how long, they have been aged. Quality can be determined up to a point by price; use the most expensive sparingly.

cider (apple cider) made from fermented apples. Available from supermarkets and health-food stores.

red wine based on fermented red wine.

white wine made from a white wine.

Conversion Chart

MEASURES

One Australian metric measuring cup holds approximately 250ml; one Australian metric tablespoon holds 20ml; one Australian metric teaspoon holds 5ml.

The difference between one country's measuring cups and another's is within a two- or three-teaspoon variance, and will not affect your cooking results. North America, New Zealand and the United Kingdom use a 15ml tablespoon.

All cup and spoon measurements are level. The most accurate way of measuring dry ingredients is to weigh them. When measuring liquids, use a clear glass or plastic jug with the metric markings.

We use large eggs with an average weight of 60g.

DRY MEASURES

METRIC	IMPERIAL
15g	½oz
30g	1oz
60g	2oz
90g	3oz
125g	4oz (¼lb)
155g	5oz
185g	6oz
220g	7oz
250g	8oz (½lb)
280g	9oz
315g	10oz
345g	11oz
375g	12oz (¾lb)
410g	13oz
440g	14oz
470g	15oz
500g	16oz (1lb)
750g	24oz (1½lb)
1kg	32oz (2lb)

LIQUID MEASURES

METRIC	IMPERIAL
30ml	1 fluid oz
60ml	2 fluid oz
100ml	3 fluid oz
125ml	4 fluid oz
150ml	5 fluid oz (¼ pint/1 gill)
190ml	6 fluid oz
250ml	8 fluid oz
300ml	10 fluid oz (½ pint)
500ml	16 fluid oz
600ml	20 fluid oz (1 pint)
1000ml (1 litre)	1¾ pints

LENGTH MEASURES

METRIC	IMPERIAL
3mm	⅛in
6mm	¼in
1cm	½in
2cm	¾in
2.5cm	1in
5cm	2in
6cm	2½in
8cm	3in
10cm	4in
13cm	5in
15cm	6in
18cm	7in
20cm	8in
23cm	9in
25cm	10in
28cm	11in
30cm	12in (1ft)

OVEN TEMPERATURES

These oven temperatures are only a guide for conventional ovens. For fan-forced ovens, check the manufacturer's manual.

	°C (CELSIUS)	°F (FAHRENHEIT)	GAS MARK
Very slow	120	250	½
Slow	150	275-300	1-2
Moderately slow	160	325	3
Moderate	180	350-375	4-5
Moderately hot	200	400	6
Hot	220	425-450	7-8
Very hot	240	475	9

Index

ACP BOOKS

General manager Christine Whiston
Editor-in-chief Susan Tomnay
Creative director & designer Hieu Chi Nguyen
Art director Hannah Blackmore
Senior editor Wendy Bryant
Additional text Xanthe Roberts
Food director Pamela Clark
Test Kitchen manager + nutritional information Belinda Farlow
Director of sales Brian Cearnes
Marketing manager Bridget Cody
Communications & brand manager Xanthe Roberts
Senior business analyst Rebecca Varela
Circulation manager Jarna Mclean
Operations manager David Scotto
Production manager Victoria Jefferys
European rights enquiries Laura Bamford lbamford@acpuk.com

ACP Books are published by ACP Magazines a division of
PBL Media Pty Limited

PBL Media, Chief Executive Officer Ian Law
Publishing & sales director, Women's lifestyle Lynette Phillips
Group editorial director, Women's lifestyle Pat Ingram
Marketing director, Women's lifestyle Matthew Dominello
Commercial manager, Women's lifestyle Seymour Cohen
Research director, Women's lifestyle Justin Stone

Produced by ACP Books, Sydney.

Published by ACP Books, a division of ACP Magazines Ltd, 54 Park St, Sydney; GPO Box 4088, Sydney, NSW 2001.
phone (02) 9282 8618; fax (02) 9267 9438. acpbooks@acpmagazines.com.au; www.acpbooks.com.au

Printed by Dai Nippon in Korea.

Australia Distributed by Network Services, phone +61 2 9282 8777; fax +61 2 9264 3278;
networkweb@networkservicescompany.com.au
United Kingdom Distributed by Australian Consolidated Press (UK), phone (01604) 642 200;
fax (01604) 642 300; books@acpuk.com
New Zealand Distributed by Netlink Distribution Company, phone (9) 366 9966; ask@ndc.co.nz
South Africa Distributed by PSD Promotions, phone (27 11) 392 6065/6/7;
fax (27 11) 392 6079/80; orders@psdprom.co.za
Canada Distributed by Publishers Group Canada
phone (800) 663 5714; fax (800) 565 3770; service@raincoast.com

Title: Classics / compiler, Pamela Clark.
ISBN: 978 1 86396 865 2 (pbk.)
Subjects: Cookery.
Other Authors/Contributors: Clark, Pamela.
Dewey Number: 641.5
© ACP Magazines Ltd 2009
ABN 18 053 273 546

Scanpan cookware is used in the AWW Test Kitchen.

Send recipe enquiries to:
recipeenquiries@acpmagazines.com.au